SELF-EDITING FOR FICTION WRITERS

SECOND EDITION

WILLIAM MORROW

An Imprint of HarperCollins*Publishers*

SELF-EDITING

FOR

FICTION WRITERS

How to Edit Yourself into Print

SECOND EDITION

RENNI BROWNE *and*

DAVE KING

ILLUSTRATIONS BY GEORGE BOOTH

HARPER

ILLUSTRATIONS FOR CHAPTERS 1 THROUGH 11
COPYRIGHT 1993 BY GEORGE BOOTH
ILLUSTRATIONS FOR CHAPTER 12: DRAWING BY BOOTH;
COPYRIGHT 1991 THE NEW YORKER MAGAZINE, INC.

HarperCollins books may be purchased for educational,
business, or sales promotional use. For information,
please e-mail the Special Markets Department at
SPsales@harpercollins.com.

Designed by Jennifer Ann Daddio

Library of Congress Cataloging-in-Publication Data

Browne, Renni.
    Self-editing for fiction writers : how to edit
yourself into print / Renni Browne and David
King.—Second ed.
        p. cm.
    Includes bibliographical references and index.
    ISBN 0-06-054569-0
    1. Fiction—Technique. 2. Editing. I. King,
Dave, 1960– II. Title.

PN162.B74 2004
808.3—dc22

                                    2003056912

16 17 18 ❖/RRD 40 39 38 37 36 35

For Ruth, who makes so much possible
—Dave King

To my son, Ross Browne
—Renni Browne

CONTENTS

Introduction to the Second Edition   *1*

1 SHOW AND TELL   *5*

2 CHARACTERIZATION AND EXPOSITION   *23*

3 POINT OF VIEW   *40*

4 PROPORTION   *67*

5 DIALOGUE MECHANICS   *82*

6 SEE HOW IT SOUNDS   *99*

7 INTERIOR MONOLOGUE   *116*

8 EASY BEATS   *140*

9 BREAKING UP IS EASY TO DO   *160*

10 ONCE IS USUALLY ENOUGH   *175*

11 SOPHISTICATION   *192*

12 VOICE   *213*

Appendix 1: Answers to Exercises   *235*

Appendix 2: Top Books for Writers   *264*

Index   *269*

About the Authors   *280*

INTRODUCTION TO
THE SECOND EDITION

There is no better way to spot room for improvement in your manuscript than by looking at it with fresh eyes. We routinely advise all writers to put their manuscripts in a drawer for a while, as a way of becoming their own fresh eyes—see chapter 4, in fact. As independent editors, we serve as the fresh eyes for our clients, giving them thoughtful feedback about problems they can't see for themselves.

Now it's our turn. Many years have passed since we launched *Self-Editing for Fiction Writers* into the world to take its place (Please, God!) next to classics for writers such as *On Becoming a Novelist, On Writing Well,* or *The Elements of Style.* During those years we've received a lot of feedback, both directly and in the form of manuscripts written by the book's fans. So we can now see room for improvement— ways in which *Self-Editing,* good as it was, could be made better. For instance, we spent a lot of time in the original edition telling you where your characters' emotions did not belong (in dialogue mechanics, for instance) and not enough time telling you where they did. As a result, we've seen a lot of overzealous writers strip their manuscripts down to an emotional minimalism that doesn't fit their story or natural style. Now we can suggest a bit more balance, making *Self-Editing* stronger than ever.

Good thing, too, because the years since the first edition have seen no change in mainstream publishing when it comes to new manuscripts receiving the editing they deserve. Strong manuscripts are still rushed into print even if they don't live up to their full potential, and manuscripts that aren't problem-free are still rejected no matter how much potential they may have. Acquisitions editors are always overworked, often undertrained, and rarely encouraged to work on manuscripts, especially since in-depth editing usually means investing time in writers who, if successful, will simply take their next book to the highest bidder. With rare exceptions, the long tradition of blue-pencil editing has passed, at least at the major publishing houses.

Among newer publishing ventures, such as on-line publishing or print on demand, the tradition never existed. These venues do offer a publishing opportunity to writers who might otherwise languish in unprinted obscurity. Unfortunately, so many writers are taking these nontraditional routes that it's far too easy to languish in printed obscurity. In order to stand out from the crowd, you need to make your manuscript as sharp as possible.

And this means self-editing. True, you can hire an independent editor to work on your manuscript. In fact, there is no better way to get the editing you need—though our opinion may be biased. But even if you do hire a pro, you want your manuscript to be as strong as it can be before you have it worked on. After all, why pay for editing you can do yourself?

You can also join a writers group and have other writers critique your manuscript. Unfortunately, writing groups can sometimes do more harm than good. Writing and editing are two different skills, and even strong writers can make poor editors. Many of these group critiques will teach you to write the book your critiquers want you to write, when you want to learn to write the book *you* want to write. The best solution is still to learn to edit yourself.

And the best way to learn editing is still from another editor, which is what you will be doing with this book. We aren't going to tell you how to plot your novel or develop your characters. What we're going to do is teach you the craft of editing. The mechanics of scene building, dialogue, point of view, interior monologue; the tricks to striking the most effective balance between narrative summary and immediate scenes; the ways to convey your characters without getting in your readers' faces; the techniques whose adoption stamps your manuscript as the work of a professional instead of an amateur. We will train you to see your manuscript as an editor might see it—to do for yourself what we most often do for our clients.

A word of warning: because writing and editing are two different skills, they require two different mind-sets. Don't try to do both at once. The time to edit is not when you're writing your first draft. But once that first draft is finished, you can use the principles in this book to increase—dramatically—the effectiveness of the story you've told and the way you've told it. You can drop your amateurish look and give your writing a professional edge.

In other words, you can edit yourself into print.

Chapter 1

SHOW AND TELL

What's wrong with this paragraph?:

> The conversation was barely begun before I
> discovered that our host was more than simply a
> stranger to most of his guests. He was an enigma, a
> mystery. And this was a crowd that doted on
> mysteries. In the space of no more than five minutes,
> I heard several different people put forth their
> theories—all equally probable or preposterous—as
> to who and what he was. Each theory was argued
> with the conviction that can only come from a lack
> of evidence, and it seemed that, for many of the
> guests, these arguments were the main reason to
> attend his parties.

In a sense, of course, there's nothing wrong. The paragraph is grammatically impeccable, and it describes the mys-

tery surrounding the party's host clearly, efficiently, and with a sense of style.

Now look at the same passage as it actually appeared in F. Scott Fitzgerald's *The Great Gatsby:*

"I like to come," Lucille said. "I never care what I do, so I always have a good time. When I was here last, I tore my gown on a chair, and he asked me my name and address—within a week I got a package from Croirier's with a new evening gown in it."

"Did you keep it?" asked Jordan.

"Sure I did. I was going to wear it tonight, but it was too big in the bust and had to be altered. It was gas blue with lavender beads. Two hundred and sixty-five dollars."

"There's something funny about a fellow that'll do a thing like that," said the other girl eagerly. "He doesn't want any trouble with *any*body."

"Who doesn't?" I inquired.

"Gatsby. Somebody told me—"

The two girls and Jordan leaned together confidentially.

"Somebody told me they thought he killed a man."

A thrill passed over all of us. The three Mr. Mumbles bent forward and listened eagerly.

"I don't think it's so much *that*," argued Lucille skeptically; "it's more that he was a German spy during the war."

One of the men nodded in confirmation.

"I heard that from a man who knew all about him,

grew up with him in Germany," he assured us positively.

"Oh, no," said the first girl, "it couldn't be that, because he was in the American army during the war." As our credulity switched back to her, she leaned forward with enthusiasm. "You look at him sometimes when he thinks nobody's looking at him. I'll bet he killed a man."

What's the difference between these two examples? To put it simply, it's a matter of showing and telling. The first version is narrative summary, with no specific settings or characters. We are simply *told* about the guests' love of mystery, the weakness of their arguments, the conviction of the arguers. In the second version we actually get to see the breathless partygoers putting forth their theories and can almost taste the eagerness of their audience. The first version is a secondhand report. The second is an immediate scene.

What, exactly, makes a scene a scene? For one thing it takes place in real time. Your readers watch events as they unfold, whether those events are a group discussion of the merits of Woody Allen films, a lone man running from an assassin, or a woman lying in a field pondering the meaning of life. In scenes, events are seen as they happen rather than described after the fact. Even flashbacks show events as they unfold, although they have unfolded in the past within the context of the story.

Scenes usually have settings as well, specific locations the readers can picture. In Victorian novels these settings were often described in exhaustive (and exhausting) detail. Nowadays literature is leaner and meaner, and it's often a good idea to give your readers just enough detail to jump-start their imaginations so they can picture your settings for themselves.

Scenes also contain some action, something that happens. Mary kills Harry, or Harry and Mary beat each other up. More often than not, what happens is dialogue between one or more characters. Though even in dialogue scenes it's a good idea to include a little physical action from time to time—what we call "beats"—to remind your readers of where your characters are and what they're doing. We'll be talking about beats at length in chapter 8.

Of course, anything that can go into a scene can also be narrated. And since scenes are usually harder to write than narration, many writers rely too heavily on narrative summary to tell their stories. The result is often page after page, sometimes chapter after chapter, of writing that reads the way the first passage quoted above reads: clearly, perhaps even stylishly, but with no specific setting, no specific characters, no dialogue.

A century or so ago this sort of writing would have been fine. It was the norm, in fact—Henry James wrote at least one entire novel composed largely of narrative summary. But thanks to the influence of movies and television, readers today have become accustomed to seeing a story as a series of immediate scenes. Narrative summary no longer engages readers the way it once did.

Since engagement is exactly what a fiction writer wants to accomplish, you're well advised to rely heavily on immediate scenes to put your story across. You want to draw your readers into the world you've created, make them feel a part of it, make them forget where they are. And you can't do this effectively if you tell your readers about your world sec-ondhand. You have to take them there.

We once worked on a novel featuring a law firm in which one of the new associates led a rebellion against the senior partners. The writer introduced the new associate and two of his colleagues in the first chapter by describing their job interviews with senior partners. The interviews were given as narrative summary—she simply told her readers what the law firm was looking for in a new associate, described the associates' backgrounds, and explained why the firm hired them. She did include snippets of dialogue from the inter-views, but since readers never found out who was speaking to the associate or where the conversations took place, there was nothing they could picture.

Knowing that the first chapter is not the best place for narrative summary—you want to engage your readers early on—we suggested that the writer turn these interviews into genuine scenes, set in the senior partner's offices, with extended conversations between the partners and the associ-ates. As a result, her readers got a much better feel for who the new associates were and a glimpse of the senior partners' humor and good nature. The book was off to a much more engaging start.

Showing your story to your readers through scenes will not only give your writing immediacy. It will give your writ-ing transparency. One of the easiest ways to look like an amateur is to use mechanics that direct attention to themselves and away from the story. You want your readers to be so wrapped up in your world that they're not even aware that you, the writer, exist. But when you switch to narrative summary, especially if you go on at length, it can sometimes seem as if you are falling into nonfiction—breaking into the story to give your readers a lecture. This is especially true if you are using narrative summary for exposition. To write exposition at length—describing your characters' pasts or events that happened before the story began or any information your readers might need to understand your plot—is to engage your readers' intellects. What you want to do is to engage their emotions.

Of course, there will be times when you need to resort to narrative summary, especially if you're writing a historical novel or science fiction, both of which usually require conveying a lot of information to your readers before you can touch their emotions. We'll talk about this in more depth in the next chapter, but for now let us say that you'd be surprised at how much exposition can be converted into scenes. Rather than describing the history of Hartsdale House, you can write a scene in which the present Lord Hartsdale points out some of the family portraits to his guests. Or rather than quoting an *Encyclopedia Galactica* article on how Llanu society is organized, you can simply drop your readers into the middle of that society and let them fend for themselves.

We once edited a book about Antonio Vivaldi, which was set, naturally, in eighteenth-century Venice. In order to follow the story the readers had to know some of the details

"Maynard constantly strives for a sense of style and immediacy."

of Venetian society in the baroque era. But because the story was presented as the reminiscences of one of Vivaldi's students, it was difficult to work the information into the text. After all, why would the student write in detail about the society she lived in? As far as she was concerned, everybody knew what the *bocca di lione* was and how you gained admission to the Golden Book.

To solve this problem, the writer created a frame story about a modern-day researcher who had found the student's writings in an archive. The researcher would interrupt the student's story every once in a while to explain some of the background. But since the researcher's explanations were simply addressed to the reader, they read like the lectures they really were. We suggested that the writer give the researcher a personality and turn his lectures into scenes.

The writer did better. In the next draft, she had cast herself in the role of the researcher, and the lectures became first-person scenes of how she was visited by the ghost of Vivaldi on a trip to Venice. Since her Vivaldi had a powerful character's voice ("That fool Mozart could roll around on the floor with the soprano between acts and no one cares. I leave the pulpit once and it follows me forever."), her tour through Venetian society took on a new life. It was shown rather than told.

Even though immediate scenes are almost always more engaging than narrative summary, be careful when self-editing not to convert *all* your narrative summary into scenes. Narrative summary has its uses, the main one being to vary the rhythm and texture of your writing. Scenes are immediate and engaging, but scene after scene without a break can become relentless and exhausting, especially if you tend to write brief, intense scenes. Every once in a while you will want to slow things down to give your readers a chance to catch their breath, and narrative summary can be a good way to do this.

One of our clients was given to short scenes in which characters met, talked, and then parted. All of the dialogue was well written and advanced his story, but since the writer delivered only five minutes' worth of dialogue in each scene, it was as if he'd written his entire novel in five-minute chunks. Reading it was like jogging on railroad ties. He could have run some of his scenes together into longer scenes, of course (and we suggested he do so), but the real solution was to use narrative summary to work some extra time into his scenes.

For instance, in the next draft he showed two characters meeting for dinner, summarized the dinner itself in a paragraph or two of narration, and then showed the five minutes of after-dinner conversation that were really crucial to the story. By simply adding a few paragraphs of narration, he stretched the duration of some of his scenes out to two or three hours without two or three hours' worth of dialogue and action. As a result his book had a more expansive feel, and his readers had a chance to breathe.

Narrative summary can also give continuity to your story on a larger scale. We recently worked on a historical novel in which the main character was forced to move to Spain during the time of the Inquisition. At first she was terrified of falling under the power of the inquisitors, but she slowly came to love the people of her new village so much that by the end of the novel, she stood up to the inquisitors in order to stay.

The writer originally tried to capture her character's

growing appreciation of her new home with a series of brief scenes spread over the several months it took for her feelings to evolve. But these short scenes lacked flow, which is especially critical at the beginning of the story. Instead, we suggested that the writer cut some of the shorter scenes and narrate the time that passed between the longer ones. Because the narrative summary was able to capture weeks or months of slow, steady growth, readers got a smooth sense of the development of the main character's feelings, with critical moments in that development illustrated by scenes. Readers could watch her feelings evolve, and that evolution invited them into the story and enabled them to identify with the heroine.

Narrative summary can also be useful when you have a lot of repetitive action. Say you are writing a book about a track star in which your hero participates in several races. If you show all of these races as immediate scenes, eventually they all start to read alike. But if you summarize the first few races—have them happen offstage, in effect—then the one you eventually show as a scene will have real impact.

And then, some plot developments are simply not important enough to justify scenes. If an event involves only minor characters, you might do better to summarize it rather than develop the characters to the point that you could write a convincing scene about them. Or if you have a minor event that leads up to a key scene, you might want to narrate the first event so that the scene, when it comes, will seem even more immediate in contrast.

We once worked on a short story in which the police

were tracking a rather enigmatic suspect. In the course of the story, three events happened in quick succession: the police realized just what the suspect was up to, they captured him, and he escaped during interrogation in a surprising way. Since the emphasis of the story was on what the suspect was up to rather than on his actual capture, we suggested that the capture be written as narrative summary. By not developing the capture into a full-blown scene, the writer was able to go almost directly from the first revelation to a second, more important revelation that comes during interrogation. The story moved at a faster pace, and the two important scenes were thrown into sharp relief because a key event between them was given as narrative summary.

So narration has a place in good fiction. Just make sure you don't use it when you should be showing rather than telling.

Up until this point, we've been talking about showing and telling on the large scale, about narrating what should be shown through immediate scenes. But even within scenes there are ways in which you may tell what you should show. The *Gatsby* scene quoted above (Fitzgerald's version) shows us how people react to Gatsby, and shows us effectively. But the writer also *tells* us that the three Mr. Mumbles leaned forward "eagerly," that one girl spoke with enthusiasm, that a man nodded "in affirmation." Granted, stylistic conventions have changed since 1925, but even so, the telling detracts because it's not needed: we've already been shown what the writer then proceeds to tell us.

Writers usually indulge in this sort of small-scale telling to put across character traits or emotions. After all, the primary aim of fiction is to get your readers so involved in the lives of your characters that they feel what your characters feel. And they can't do that unless you make your characters' feelings clear. So you tell them. "Bishop Pettibone was never a man to allow his religion to interfere with his private life." "Wilbur felt absolutely defeated." "Geraldine was horrified at the news."

But telling your readers about your characters' emotions is not the best way to get your readers involved. Far better to show why your characters feel the way they do. Instead of saying "Amanda took one look at the hotel room and recoiled in disgust," describe the room in such a way that the readers feel that disgust for themselves. You don't want to give your readers information. You want to give them experiences.

It's more work that way, of course. It's easier simply to say "Erma was depressed" than to come up with some original bit of action or interior monologue that shows she's depressed. But if you have her take one bite of her favorite cake and push the rest away—or polish off the whole cake—you will have given your readers a far better feel for her depression than you could by simply describing it. People are depressed—or angry or relieved—in their own unique ways, so simply conveying the fact of the emotion to your readers doesn't really tell them who your character is. It's nearly always best to resist the urge to explain. Or, as we so often write it in manuscript margins, *R.U.E.*

This tendency to describe a character's emotion may reflect a lack of confidence on the part of the writer. And more often than not, writers tell their readers things already shown by dialogue and action. It's as if they're repeating themselves to make sure their readers get the point. So when you come across an explanation of a character's emotion, simply cut the explanation. If the emotion is still shown, then the explanation wasn't needed. If the emotion isn't shown, rewrite the passage so that it is.

To show you what we mean, take one last look at the Fitzgerald scene, this time with the explanations taken out. (We've also made a few other editorial changes using the principles you'll be learning later in the book.) You can see from the results just how good a job Fitzgerald did in showing all the emotions he tagged for us unnecessarily:

"I like to come," Lucille said. "I never care what I do, so I always have a good time. When I was here last, I tore my gown on a chair, and he asked me my name and address—within a week I got a package from Croirier's with a new evening gown in it."

"Did you keep it?" Jordan asked.

"Sure I did. I was going to wear it tonight, but it was too big in the bust and had to be altered. It was gas blue with lavender beads. Two hundred and sixty-five dollars."

"There's something funny about a fellow that'll do a thing like that," said the other girl. "He doesn't want any trouble with *any*body."

"Who doesn't?" I said.

"Gatsby. Somebody told me—"

The two girls and Jordan leaned their heads together.

"Somebody told me that they thought he killed a man."

A thrill passed over all of us. The three Mr. Mumbles bent forward in their seats.

"I don't think it's so much *that*," Lucille said. "It's more that he was a German spy during the war."

One of the men nodded. "I heard that from a man who knew all about him, grew up with him in Germany."

"Oh, no," said the first girl, "it couldn't be that, because he was in the American army during the war. You look at him sometimes when he thinks nobody's looking at him. I'll bet he killed a man."

Even within descriptions that have nothing to do with character emotion, there are ways you can show rather than tell. Rather than telling your readers that your hero's car is an old broken-down wreck, you can show him twisting two bare wires together to turn on the headlights or driving through a puddle and being sprayed from the holes in the floor. That way your readers can draw their own conclusions about the car's condition.

And just to show that editors aren't the only ones who notice showing and telling imbalances, here's a quote from Frederick Busch's *Los Angeles Times* review of Peter Ackroyd's *Dickens: Life and Times*:

The need to announce, along with a need to reinforce with comment what has just been clearly shown, results in tones more appropriate to Dickens' funnier re-creations of his father's pomposities: "So far had the young author already come . . ."; "So did the real world enter Dickens' fiction . . ."; "So did his life, interior and exterior, continue. . . ." Where was Ackroyd's editor?

Bear in mind that "show, don't tell," is not a hard-and-fast rule. (In fact, none of the self-editing principles in this book should be treated as rules.) There are going to be times when telling will create more engagement than showing. In the Fitzgerald passage, for instance, the line "A thrill passed over all of us" is clearly telling. And yet this line, coming so close on the rumor that Gatsby may have killed a man, gives a flavor of cheap gossip to the scene that heightens its effect.

But in good fiction this sort of telling is the exception, and a rare exception at that. Because when you show your story rather than tell it, you treat your readers with respect. And that respect makes it easier for you to draw them into the world you've created.

Checklist

- How often do you use narrative summary? Are there long passages where nothing happens in real time? Do

the main events in your plot take place in summary or
in scenes?

- If you do have too much narrative summary, which
sections do you want to convert into scenes? Does any
of it involve major characters, where a scene could be
used to flesh out their personalities? Does any of your
narrative summary involve major plot twists or
surprises? If so, start writing some scenes.

- Do you have *any* narrative summary, or are you
bouncing from scene to scene without pausing for
breath?

- Are you describing your characters' feelings? Have
you *told* us they're angry? irritated? morose?
discouraged? puzzled? excited? happy? elated?
suicidal? Keep an eye out for any places where you
mention an emotion outside of dialogue. Chances are
you're telling what you should show. Remember to
R.U.E.

Exercises

*Spot the telling in the following and convert it to showing. The
answers (at least, our answers) appear at the back of the book.*

A.   "Mortimer? Mortimer?" Simon Hedges said.
"Where are you?"

"Look up, you ninny. I'm on the roof."

"What in blazes are you doing perched up there?"

Mortimer Twill explained to Simon how his long-awaited cupola and weather vane had finally arrived. He just couldn't wait for Simon to install the gadgets, so Mortimer had decided to climb up to the roof and complete the installation himself. He was still sorting through the directions.

"Come on down before you kill yourself," Simon said. "I swear I'll put them up for you this afternoon."

B.   I'd known Uncle Zeb for years, of course, but I didn't feel like I really knew him until that first time I walked into his shop. All that time I'd thought he was just kind of handy, but looking at his tools—hundreds of them—and what they were and the way they were organized, well, I could see he was a craftsman.

If you're in an ambitious mood, take the following bit of narrative summary and convert it into a scene. Hint: feel free to create any characters or elaborate on the settings.

C.   Once you got off Route 9W, though, you were in another world, a world where two streets never met at a right angle, where streets, in fact, didn't exist. Instead you had "courts," "terraces," "ways," a "landing" or two. And lining these street-like things were row on row of little houses that could be distinguished, it seemed, only by the lawn ornaments. Travelers who disappeared into the developments had been known to call taxis just to lead them out again.

Chapter 2

CHARACTERIZATION
AND EXPOSITION

Eloise had always assumed she would grow up to live like her mother—a quiet, sensible life full of furniture wax, good nutritious breakfasts, and compulsive bed making. But her first college roommate, Randi, introduced her to a whole new world, a world where you didn't have to tidy up before you invited friends in, where you didn't have to squeeze the toothpaste carefully from the bottom, and where you didn't have to pick up an iron for the rest of your natural life. Eloise felt like she had been granted a reprieve after eighteen years in the June Cleaver Institute for Neurotic Young Girls.

Now, after spending ten minutes rooting through a pile of clothes to find a blouse that wasn't too dirty, then crunching across the living room carpet to spend another five hunting up a clean cereal bowl, she began to think that maybe there was something to be said for her mother's lifestyle.

After reading these paragraphs, you know something—possibly something important—about Eloise, her personality and background. But do you care? Most readers will probably be unable to work up more than the mildest interest in this character the writer is working so hard to put over.

You're likely to have spotted the culprit—there's a lot of narrative summary in that first paragraph—and may already have thought of a way to convert this material into a scene (you could have Eloise's mother make a surprise visit, for instance). And, yes, one of the problems with this passage is that it tells us what it could be showing. In fact, the show-and-tell principle underlies many of the self-editing points we talk about from now on. But there's a second problem here: the writer introduces Eloise to his readers all at once and in depth—stopping the story cold for an overview of her character.

A lot of writers seem to feel they have to give their readers a clear understanding of a new character before they can get on with their story. They never bring a character on-stage without a brief personality summary. Or else they introduce their characters with flashbacks to the childhood scenes that made them who they are—in effect, psychoanalyzing the characters for their readers.

It's often a good idea to introduce a new character with enough physical description for your readers to picture him or her. As with describing your settings, all you need are a few concrete, idiomatic details to jump-start your readers' imaginations ("A good-looking man in his fifties," for instance, is too vague to be interesting). But when it comes to your characters' personalities, it's much more engaging to have these emerge from character action, reaction, interior monologue, and dialogue than from description.

For instance, watching Eloise fish for clean clothes and crunch across her carpet is enough to tell us she's a slob. We don't need to know at this point how she became one. Later in the story, we could learn about her upbringing when her mother comes to visit. In other words, we could get to know Eloise slowly, with all the attendant pleasure of gradual discovery, the way we would get to know her in real life.

Another reason to avoid thumbnail character sketches is that the personality traits you tell us about when you introduce a character will (we would hope) eventually be shown by the way the character behaves in the story. After all, if you describe a character as an elegant society matron and then show her flicking food at her husband in a restaurant or picking her nose in church, your readers won't believe your description. If your characters actually act the way your summaries say they will, the summaries aren't needed. If they don't, the summaries are misleading. Either way, your fiction is likely to be much more effective without the character summary.

Also, when you sum up your characters, you risk defining them to the point that they're boxed in by the characterization with no room to grow. Someone once asked Leonard Nimoy how he came to develop the complex relationship between Captain Kirk and Mr. Spock that was one of the chief strengths of the old *Star Trek* series. How had he gone about working out such a deep and authentic friendship beforehand? Nimoy simply said that he hadn't—and in fact couldn't have—worked it out in advance. Had he consciously mapped out Spock's relationship with Kirk, that relationship would never have been any deeper than the plan he had worked out. Instead he played the character intuitively, and there was no limit to the depth the relationship could attain.

When you define your characters the minute you introduce them, you may be setting boundary lines that your readers will use to interpret your characters' actions through the rest of the book. But if you allow your readers to get to know your characters gradually, each reader will interpret them in his or her own way, thus getting a deeper sense of who your characters are than you could ever convey in a summary. Allowing your readers this sort of leeway in understanding your characters enables you to reach a wider audience—and reach it far more effectively—than would defining your characters before we get to know them or analyzing them afterward.

Finally, sketching out your characters for your readers is just plain obtrusive. It's a form of telling that is almost certain to make your readers aware that you the writer are hard at work.

Some writers take a more subtle approach than simply describing a new character's personality—they describe each new character's history. In the course of the story, they may even trace their characters' ancestry back two or three generations. It's perfectly understandable that a writer should undertake this sort of historical characterization. Delving

"The dwarf! The dwarf! The damn dwarf hiding in the foot locker! A hundred pages, or so ago! What was his name?..."

into a character's past can be a good way for you to understand the character in the present. But though it may have been helpful for you to write a character's history, it may not be necessary for your readers to read it. Once you understand a character well enough to bring him or her to life, we don't have to know where the character came from.

Also, since the easiest way to bring out a character's history is through flashback, and since you bring your present story to a halt whenever you start a flashback, it doesn't take many flashbacks to make your present-time story jerky or hard to follow. So if you find your story too heavily burdened with the past, consider letting some of the past go. The characterization you draw from the flashback may not be needed, or you may be able to find a way to bring it out in the present.

We recently worked on a book about a superficially happy man in his early forties who begins to explore his past after his second marriage fails. He starts out in an attempt to win his ex-wife back and in the end discovers that several people around him, including his closest friends, are not who he thought they were. The story of the hero's past, which included a bizarrely abusive mother, is critical to the plot, and the writer brought it out in a series of very well written flashbacks.

The problem was that the writer gave us flashbacks of the ex-wife's past, of the hero's father's childhood, and of the life of some of the hero's childhood friends. In the middle of the book, the writer included six chapters in a row made up entirely of flashbacks with a paragraph or two at the beginning and end to give the flashback a frame—the hero's present life simply disappeared for more than a hundred pages. We suggested that the writer cut all but the most essential flashbacks and let us get to know his characters in the present rather than in the past.

So how do you go about establishing a character gradually and unobtrusively? The art of establishing a character is a large enough topic to make a book in itself, but there are some techniques that fall within the area of fiction mechanics. You can have one character characterized by another instead of by the writer. Rather than writing, "Cuthbert was not the sort of person whom others were drawn to immediately," you can have one of your characters say, "Like most people, I disliked Cuthbert on first sight."

Also, you can develop your character through dialogue and "beats" (descriptions of physical action. We'll cover both of these topics in considerable detail later. For now, if you want to learn who someone really is, watch what they say and do. And if you want your readers to get a feel for who your characters really are, show them to us through dialogue and action.

Another unobtrusive way to develop a character is to write not about the character directly but about other matters from that character's viewpoint. This amounts to your giving us your character's views of the world rather than your views of your character. We'll get into this in more depth in the following chapter, but for now consider the opening paragraph of Graham Greene's *Monsignor Quixote:*

It happened this way: Father Quixote had ordered his solitary lunch from his housekeeper and set off to buy wine at a local cooperative eight kilometers away from El Toboso on the main road to Valencia. It was a day when the heat stood and quivered on the dry fields, and there was no air conditioning in the little Seat 600 he had bought, already second hand, eight years before. As he drove he thought sadly of the day when he would have to find a new car. A dog's years can be multiplied by seven to equal a man's, and by that calculation his car would still be in early middle age, but he noticed how already his parishioners began to regard his Seat as almost senile. "You can't trust it, Don Quixote," they would warn him, and he could only reply, "It has been with me through many bad days, and I pray God that it may survive me." So many of his prayers had remained unanswered that he had hopes this one prayer of his had lodged all the time like wax in the Eternal ear.

This characterization is not particularly gradual. We have known Father Quixote for all of one paragraph, but by its end we know quite a lot about him, his circumstances, his turn of mind, his sense of humor. But notice that Greene says absolutely nothing about Quixote himself. He talks about the priest's car, his parishioners, his prayer life, not about his character. Yet because we get all of this information from Quixote's point of view, the priest is there before us.

And we get to recognize him for ourselves, making our own judgments about his personality. When you present your readers with already-arrived-at conclusions about your characters, you leave your readers with nothing to do, and passive readers are at best unengaged and at worst bored. You need to let your readers take an active role in the writer-reader partnership to draw them into your story.

Everything we've said about characterization applies to exposition as well. Background, backstory (what happened before the story begins), the information your readers need in order to follow and appreciate your plot—all these should be brought out as unobtrusively as possible. When you give your readers all of your exposition all at once, you're likely to be feeding them more information than they can absorb. And unless you're John le Carré, you can't get by with forcing readers to flip pages back and forth in order to follow your story. Not to mention the risk you run of lecturing your readers. A good rule of thumb is to give your readers only as much background information, or history, or characterization, as they need at any given time.

The theory and practice of circumventing burglar alarms was a major part of the plot in a client's police procedural. In the first draft, the writer included nearly an entire chapter on how the various types of burglar alarms work and how they can be defeated—which, of course, effectively stopped his story short while he delivered a lecture. In his second draft he worked the same information in at various places throughout the book, giving readers just as much burglar-alarm theory as they needed to know at any given point.

The most obtrusive type of exposition is, of course, a long discourse in the narrative voice, like the how-to on burglar alarms. As you'll remember from the first chapter, these blocks of what is essentially nonfiction can usually be converted into immediate scenes. But just because exposition takes place in a scene doesn't necessarily mean it's unobtrusive. A few decades ago most stage plays opened with what they called "a feather duster." The maid (carrying a feather duster) would walk on the stage and answer a conveniently placed telephone:

> Hello? . . . No, Master Reginald isn't here. He and Mistress Elmira went to the airport to pick up his brother Zack, who disappeared twenty years ago with half the family fortune and has now been found living in the Andes. . . . What? No, young Master Roderick isn't here either. He and his young lady, Faith Hubberthwait-Jones, have gone off to see his solicitor about the possibility of opening the trust left to him by Great-Uncle Fornsby. . . . Yes, she is Lord Hubberthwait-Jones's daughter—a fine old family, but not a penny to their name. . . . No, I'm afraid Blump, the groundskeeper, isn't here either. He's running the prize hound, Artaxerxes, in the Chipping Sodbury Meet in hopes of winning enough to cover his gambling debts. . . . Yes, thank you, I'll tell them you called.

Technically this sort of thing is dialogue, but it doesn't sound like anything anyone on this planet, in this century, would actually say. It *is* possible to get exposition across unobtrusively through dialogue, but when your characters start talking solely for the sake of informing your readers, the exposition gets in the way of believable characterization. So be on the lookout for places where your dialogue is actually exposition in disguise.

The same holds true for interior monologue. We once worked on a historical mystery set in a sixteenth-century convent. At one point, the main character simply sat in her room and pondered such everyday details of convent life as why the sisters were given the rooms they occupied. Technically it was interior monologue, but it was also out of character—people simply don't sit around and think about everyday details of their lives. In the writer's next draft a new sister arrived at the convent and complained that her room was too small, and the information came out naturally in a scene.

Or consider this scene, taken from a novel we edited a few years ago. The point of view is that of a church organist, sitting at her console and watching mourners file in for a funeral service:

She might've known Fitzhugh Jordan would be there. Some nerve, after all he did to keep that girl from coming home for Christmas. And just look at him, slipping into that pew beside his daddy, sweet as Gabriel blowing his horn. She was surprised Peter Griffith would let him in the church; then again, she wasn't, considering.

Peter and Melinda Griffith were the last ones. And not a minute too soon. Mary Lou was about to run out of music and have to repeat herself.

Peter walked right close to Melinda, though there could've been a wall of glass between them for all the contact they made. But Mary Lou had to admit they made a handsome couple—Peter tall and dark like an Italian movie star, Melinda blond and sweet-looking, though looks do lie.

Melinda looked *wounded,* that was the only word for it. Hands fluttering, eyes glancing off people's faces like moths off a window.

The two of them followed Fitzhugh into the family pew, which meant Mary Lou could finally wind down.

She thought she'd close with "Abide with Me."

Once again, the writer uses interior monologue to bring out the recent history of the Jordan family in these paragraphs—Fitzhugh's opposition to "that girl" (whose identity is clear in the context), Peter and Melinda's lost love, Melinda's pain. And it all comes to the reader so unobtrusively. Mary Lou is such a credible character, and this material is so much *in* character, that none of this exposition feels like exposition. We take in the information not just painlessly but with real pleasure.

Again, just to prove that other people besides editors notice cumbersome exposition, here is a quote from Robert Stuart Nathan's review of Victor O'Reilly's *Games of the Hangman:*

The novel's other sins include vast passages of irrelevant exposition; people ignorant of common facts, such as the police official who says the dead boy was "from a place called Bern," only to have Hugo obligingly respond, "It's the Swiss capital," and characters awkwardly informing each other of things they already know, solely for the reader's benefit, as when one character asks, "Do you know the story of the original Alibe?" and Hugo replies, "Remind me."

Perhaps the toughest exposition challenge is introducing your readers to a new culture. This could be something as simple as conveying everyday life in rural Tennessee to readers who may live in Palm Beach (or vice versa). Or you may have to re-create the sense of life in Restoration London or twelfth-century Paris or second-century Rome. In a science fiction or fantasy novel, it might involve conveying an ancient culture based on an alien biology living on a world with a unique geology. And your readers need to be in that culture from the start of your story. How do you transport your readers to strange new worlds without loading down your opening with a lot of exposition?

Bear in mind that this kind of background is really characterization, only what's being characterized is a culture rather than a person. And as was the case with characterization, readers can best learn about your locations and backgrounds not through lengthy exposition but by seeing them in real life.

Consider, for instance, the opening scene from Diana Wynne Jones's *Dogsbody:*

> The Dog Star stood beneath the Judgment Seats and raged. The green light of his fury fired the assembled faces viridian. It lit the underside of the rooftrees and turned their moist blue fruit to emerald.
>
> "None of this is *true!*" he shouted. "Why can't you believe *me,* instead of listening to *him?*" He blazed on the chief witness, a blue luminary from the Castor

complex, firing him turquoise. The witness backed hastily out of range.

"Sirius," the First Judge rumbled quietly, "we've already found you guilty. Unless you've anything reasonable to say, be quiet and let the Court pass sentence."

"No I will *not* be quiet!" Sirius shouted up at the huge ruddy figure. He was not afraid of Antares. He had often sat beside him as Judge on those same Judgment Seats—that was one of the many miserable things about this trial. "You haven't listened to a word I've said, all through. I did *not* kill that luminary—I only hit him. I was *not* negligent, and I've offered to look for the Zoi. The most you can accuse me of is losing my temper—"

"Once too often, in the opinion of this Court," remarked big crimson Betelgeuse, the Second Judge, in his dry way.

"And I've admitted I lost my temper," said Sirius.

"No one would have believed you if you hadn't," said Betelgeuse.

A long flicker of amusement ran around the assembled luminaries. Sirius glared at them. The hall of blue trees was packed with people from every sphere and all orders of effulgence. It was not often one of the high effulgents was on trial for his life—and there never had been one so notorious for losing his temper.

It takes a lot of self-confidence to drop readers into the middle of the trial of a star god by a council of his peers and leave so much unexplained—readers never see the hall of blue trees again, for instance, and we don't learn what a Zoi is until near the end of the novel. And yet, this approach works, in part because the emotions are so powerful that readers are drawn into the story despite the unanswered questions. Indeed, finding the answers is one of the things that keeps readers reading. Also, by never explaining her situations, by trusting her readers to keep up with her, Jones pays her readers the compliment of assuming them to be intelligent.

And that's a compliment any writer would do well to pass along.

Checklist

- Look back over a scene or chapter that introduces one or more characters. How much time, if any, have you spent describing the new characters' character? Are you telling us about characteristics that will later show up in dialogue and action?
- How about character histories? How many of your characters' childhoods have you developed in detail? Can some of these life stories be cut?
- What information (technical details, characters' past histories, backgrounds on locations or families) do your readers need in order to understand your story? At what point in the story do they need to know it?

- How are you getting this information across to your readers? Have you given it to them all at once through a short writer-to-reader lecture (see exercise B)?
- If the exposition comes out through dialogue, is it through dialogue your characters would actually speak even if your readers didn't have to know the information? In other words, does the dialogue exist only to put the information across?

Exercises

A.   *How would you develop the following character through a series of scenes? Keep in mind that the scenes don't have to be consecutive and that some of the material need not be included at all.*

Maggie had reached the cusp of her childhood, that gray area between girl and woman when she could be either, neither, or both almost at will. There had not been (and probably would not be) a lonelier time in her life. She could no longer associate with children, whose interests now bored her. But she wasn't comfortable with adults, for she still carried the energy of a child and couldn't slow herself down to the adults' pace.

And so she found herself trapped between the banal and the dull, trying to shape her life with only the help of her contemporaries, who were as adrift as she was. Given all this, was it any wonder she sometimes seemed, well, exasperated (and exasperating) to her parents?

B.   *Now try the same thing with a passage of exposition.*

The county had changed over the years. It had all started with the George Washington Bridge, which finally put the west side of the Hudson within commuting distance of New York City without the bother of trains and ferries. Then had come the Tappan Zee Bridge, a second artery running right through the heart of the county. It was only a matter of time before the family farms were turned into developments and the little two-lane roads became four-lane highways.

Fred could remember when Nanuet had only one traffic light. Now it had a string of twelve of them on Route 59 alone, mostly in front of the mall. (The Mall!) And Route 59 itself was well on its way to becoming a continuous string of malls and shopping centers, all the way from Nyack to Suffern and beyond. It had reached the point where shoppers outnumbered residents three to one on a busy day.

Chapter 3

POINT OF VIEW

"Want some buttermilk?" July asked, going to the crock.

"No, sir," Joe said. He hated buttermilk, but July loved it so that he always asked anyway.

"You ask him that every night," Elmira said from the edge of the loft. It irritated her that July came home and did exactly the same things day after day.

"Stop asking him," she said sharply. "Let him get his own buttermilk if he wants any. It's been four months now and he ain't drunk a drop—looks like you'd let it go."

She spoke with a heat that surprised July. Elmira could get angry about almost anything, it seemed. Why would it matter if he invited the boy to have a drink of buttermilk? All he had to do was say no, which he had.

Larry McMurtry's *Lonesome Dove* is a powerfully written book, yet some readers find it hard to get involved in the story, in part because of passages like the above. The characters are clear, the dialogue has an authentic feel, but in the second paragraph we're seeing the scene as Joe sees it, in the third we've switched to Elmira, and in the last paragraph we've switched again, to July. We never settle into a single point of view.

Some writing books distinguish as many as twenty-six different flavors of point of view, but there are really only three basic approaches: first person, third person, and omniscient. The first person is the "I" voice, where all the narration is written as if the narrator were speaking directly to the readers. ("I knew as soon as I entered the room that something was wrong, but it was a few seconds before I realized the stuffed moose was missing.") Note that in first person the narrator is one of the characters, not the writer.

The first-person point of view has a number of advantages, the main one being that it gives your readers a great deal of intimacy with your viewpoint character. When you are writing in the "I" voice, your main character effortlessly invites your readers into his or her head and shows them the world through his or her eyes. Consider the following example, adapted from a submission to one of our workshops:

> I never did think I'd see the day when I was
> thankful for the oak.
> I certainly wasn't thankful this last autumn when I
> stood with my rake in the middle of the scraggly

patches of grass that pass for the front lawn and cursed the leaves that, I swear, multiplied like loaves and fishes on their way to the ground. Come autumn, I'll probably stand and curse the tree again.

But for now, when it seems the dog days have come to linger, when the sun'd bake anyone fool enough to venture off his porch and onto the street—well, that tree is a positive comfort.

Or consider the introduction to the title character in Sharyn McCrumb's *The Ballad of Frankie Silver:*

They have brought me down from my beautiful mountain in the white silence of winter, my wrists bound with hemp rope, my legs tied beneath the pony's belly as if I were a yearling doe taken on the long hunt. And perhaps I am, for I am as defenseless as a deer, and as silent. They say that deer, who live out their lives in silence, scream when they are killed. Well, perhaps I will be permitted that.

Of course, in order to succeed in the first-person point of view, you have to create a character strong enough and interesting enough to keep your readers going for an entire novel, yet not so eccentric or bizarre that your readers feel trapped inside his or her head. Also, what you gain in intimacy with the first person, you lose in perspective. You can't write about anything your main character couldn't know, which means you have to have your main character on the spot whenever you want to write an immediate scene. This can limit your plot-development possibilities.

Also, when you write your entire novel from one point of view, your readers get to know only one character directly. Everyone else is filtered through your viewpoint character. One way around this is to write in the first person but from several different viewpoints—with different scenes done from inside the heads of different characters. This technique can be highly effective in the hands of an experienced writer. For instance, over the course of Sol Stein's *The Best Revenge,* first-person sections are written from the points of view of six different characters. And Mary Gordon devotes the last section in *The Company of Women* to first-person accounts by all the major characters in turn.

At the other end of the spectrum from the first person is the omniscient point of view. Instead of being written from inside the head of one of your characters, a scene in the omniscient point of view is not written from inside anyone's head. (Note: Some writing books consider scenes that dip into different heads, as in the *Lonesome Dove* quote, to be omniscient narration. We have another take on this technique, but more about that below.) You may think of omniscient narration as a nineteenth-century technique. ("It was the best of times, it was the worst of times," or, "It is a truth universally acknowledged that a single man in possession of a good fortune must be in want of a wife.") And it's true that the omniscient point of view reached its most extreme form in nineteenth-century novels such as George

Eliot's *Middlemarch,* in which the writer pauses the action to address the reader directly:

> If you want to know more particularly how Mary looked, ten to one you will see a face like hers in the crowded street tomorrow, if you are there on the watch: she will not be among those daughters of Zion who are haughty, and walk with stretched-out necks and wanton eyes, mincing as they go. Let all those pass, and fix your eyes on some small plump brownish person of firm but quiet carriage, who looks about her, but does not suppose that anybody is looking at her.

You're unlikely to want to go as far as this—it's difficult to maintain transparency when you're having a chat with your readers—but the omniscient point of view in its milder forms does have its uses. A number of writers, from Joyce Carol Oates to Douglas Adams, have written successfully using the omniscient point of view.

Consider these paragraphs from Jane Langton's *Divine Inspiration.* Earlier, through scenes, she has established the necessity of groundwater beneath a church in order to keep its wooden supporting pilings intact in the soft soil on which it has been built. She has also established the existence of a sump pump designed to drain a construction site across the street:

> One day a car pulled up beside the excavation. A court hack jumped out, skidded down the slope and handed the job engineer an order to cease and desist. The engineer looked at the piece of paper, threw up his

"The Rapid Express man is here with your manuscript. He says you have too many points of view from too many characters. He says all these jumps are distracting, to say the least."

hands, bellowed at the crane operator and the guy working the power shovel to get the hell home, leaped into his car and careened away from the curb and the excavation and the whole job of building a five-story hotel with Georgian exterior and luxury interior fittings, raced home and burst in on his wife, fuming and steaming, to find her *in flagrante* with his best friend, and in the succeeding uproar and confusion the little matter of the necessity of turning off the sump pump under the excavation at the corner of Commonwealth and Clarendon utterly vanished from his mind.

The neglected pump had long since sucked the excavation dry. Now it was pumping groundwater, relentlessly draining the saturated soil at level four, sending the water pulsing into a pipe to be carried by way of the West Side Interceptor to a pumping station and a treatment plant and eventual discharge into Boston Harbor. It was gone for good.

Since none of Langton's characters are aware of the pump, this is clearly written from the omniscient point of view. Yet the pump's abandonment ultimately leads to the collapse of the church, which plays out in a spectacular, climactic scene at the end. Langton builds toward this climax with a number of scenes about the deterioration of the pilings, all written from the omniscient perspective, that work on the reader like ominous background music throughout the novel.

Note that with the omniscient voice what you gain in perspective you lose in intimacy. Take a look at the workshop passage we quoted earlier, rewritten as omniscient narration:

In small South Carolina towns, most houses are built in the shadow of tall trees. Each autumn, the children charged with the yard care curse the leaves that seem to multiply on their way to the ground. But on particular mid-afternoons during the dog days of August, when the blazing sun had taken possession of the streets and baked anyone who dared to challenge it, entire families retreated to their front porches, there to await whatever stray breezes happened by in the shade of those same trees.

One such tree, a tall oak, stood in the front yard of the house Coral Blake rented from a man who had long ago moved his family north. The lush expanse of the oak belied the barren nature of the surrounding yard, where little grew except sparse clumps of grass, random weeds, and a scraggly pair of hydrangea bushes—pale blue instead of violet.

This passage contains more information than the previous version, but it lacks the warmth, the sense of what it actually feels like to sit under an old oak tree in the dog days.

Then there is the third person. If the first person invites intimacy and the omniscient narrator allows for perspective, the third person strikes a balance between the two. Actually, it can strike any number of balances—it's the attempt to define precisely these various degrees of intimacy versus perspective that leads the obsessive to describe twenty-six different flavors of point of view. It's much less complicated simply to treat the third-person point of view as a continuum, running from narrative intimacy to narrative distance.

What determines where your writing falls on the continuum? Perhaps the most basic factors are your word choice and syntax. The words we have at our disposal to describe the world arise out of our history, our education, our culture, even our weather, which is why the Inuit have so many words for snow and the Irish so many phrases for a rainy day. When you describe your settings and action using only words from your viewpoint character's vocabulary, you're not only telling your readers the facts, you're running those facts through your viewpoint character's history and sensibility. On the other hand, when the voice of your descriptions is more sophisticated, more verbose, perhaps more acutely observant than your viewpoint character can manage, you've put distance between the two.

Let's take another look at Coral, third person, but in her own words:

> Coral Blake mopped the gritty sweat out of her eyes and gazed up at the dusty green underside of the oak. The dog days of August had settled in, it seemed, and like most folks in Greeleyville, South Carolina, she took cover from the sun on her front porch under that grandfatherly tree.
>
> My, how she hated that tree in the autumn. Then, she'd stand out in the scraggly front yard with a rake and curse the leaves that multiplied like loaves and fishes as they fell. But now, with her head up against the cool metal of the glider, the tree was a positive blessing.

And one final look, from a little more distance:

Coral Blake mopped the sweat out of her eyes and gazed up at the dusty green underside of the oak. It seemed the dog days of August had arrived, and like most of the citizens of Greeleyville, South Carolina, she took refuge from the sun on her front porch under the tree.

Ironic how much she hated that tree at other times. Every fall she'd stand in her threadbare front yard with a rake and curse the leaves that multiplied as they fell. But now, resting her head against the cool metal of the glider, she considered the tree to be a blessing.

Or notice how much of Little Lucien's life experience comes through in this brief description of a summer's evening from Carolyn Chute's *Letourneau's Used Auto Parts:*

June bugs growl like bulldozers in the corners of Big Lucien Letourneau's slanty old piazza and the old twisty tree-sized lilac bushes put off a smell. Big Lucien is nowhere around tonight. Norman is not around. Little Lucien is squatted with his back against the clapboards, his eyes closed, listening to the tantes whisper in French just inside the screen door . . . something about the gas stove, he surmises.

Even though it's not clear we're in Little Lucien's head until near the end of the paragraph, his view of life is already there in the comparison of June bugs to bulldozers and the way lilacs "put off" a smell. It's the language that makes the writing intimate.

Another factor that controls your narrative distance is how much you allow your viewpoint character's emotions to color your descriptions. Say, for instance, you're writing a description of a New England snowstorm. If your main character is a middle-aged man who has cleared the driveway twice that week and is already walking the dog on snowshoes, then you might describe the snow as falling "slowly and inexorably, smothering the landscape." If your viewpoint character is a little girl delighting in her first real winter, you might describe the snow "floating gently down and making the yard fresh and new again." Same facts, different feelings, different descriptions. If, on the other hand, your writing is emotionally detached, then, well, your writing is emotionally detached.

So what degree of narrative distance is right for you? Broadly speaking, the more intimate the point of view, the better. One of the most vital and difficult tasks facing a writer is creating believable and engaging characters, and an intimate point of view is a terrific way to do this. When you use your characters' language in your descriptions, you not only convey the sights and sounds around them, you also convey their history, their education, and the culture they live in, without any additional effort. If one collegiate character watches an old Mustang go by and hears a "loud motor," and another hears a "302 Windsor with Holly duals and glasspacks," an astute reader can guess at how they spent their respective high school years.

Allowing your characters' emotions to steep into your descriptions also lets you use description more freely. When your descriptions simply convey information to your readers, they interrupt the story and slow the pace down. To avoid this, many writers pare description down to a bare minimum, often leaving their writing sterile and their pace overly uniform. When description also conveys a character's personality or mood, you can use it to vary your pace or add texture without interrupting the flow. The description itself advances the story.

Also, writing with narrative intimacy lets you convey a wide range of emotions, including some so subtle that your viewpoint character may not even be aware of them. This can be a powerful corrective for writers who take the first chapter's "show, don't tell," advice too much to heart, stripping all hint of emotion out of their narrative for fear of slipping into purple prose. The result is often writing that is cold and spare, if not worse. The emotions have to go somewhere, and the language of your descriptions is a good place for them.

We once had a client who tried to convey nearly all of his characters' emotion through dialogue and interior monologue. As a result, his characters felt only the most self-conscious, intrusive emotions—primarily anger, fear, and lust, which wore his readers down after a while. He had to learn to allow his viewpoint character's mood to color the narration before he could capture ennui, anticipation, contentment, and a host of subtler feelings.

Though you will almost always want narrative intimacy, especially if you're writing from the viewpoint of a major character, sometimes there are good reasons for maintaining narrative distance. If you want your readers to focus more on the action of a scene than on the personalities involved in it, for instance, you might want to keep the narrative voice more impersonal. Or, if you need to write a scene from the viewpoint of a minor character, you don't want to present your readers with a well-rounded, fully developed worldview, lest they assume the character is more important than he or she actually is. If you want to describe a situation or state of mind that is beyond your viewpoint character's vocabulary—because your character is uneducated or a child, for instance—then you might need to write with more narrative distance. If your viewpoint character is a psychotic killer, you may want to write his scenes using a more neutral, distant voice. After all, you want to engage your readers, not drive them to distraction.

The most important thing is to maintain control of your narrative distance, to use it deliberately to do what you need to do in a given scene. And this is why it's almost always important to stick with a single viewpoint throughout a given scene—to decide which character's viewpoint you are going to use, get into that characters' head, and stay there until the scene is over. Even if you're writing with greater narrative distance, you would still describe only what your viewpoint character could see and hear. When you jump from head to head, as in the *Lonesome Dove* example, you're trying to achieve narrative intimacy with all your characters at once, and readers will almost always find that more confusing than engaging.

Consider the following scene from a client's submission, in which Markey has just informed Mrs. Blake that her son is dead:

"What happened?" She was standing under the archway to the living room, staring at him.

Markey looked up. Apparently she was going to be trouble.

"He was in a kayak," he said.

"A kayak. I see." She stepped back into the room. "Then he drowned?"

"Yes, Mrs. Blake, we assume so."

"What do you mean, you assume so?" Her voice began to rise. "How can you stand there and tell me you assume so? Who are you?"

"Clayton Markey, ma'am."

She could feel his discomfort at being on the other side of a question.

The second paragraph in this example ("Apparently she was going . . .") is clearly from Markey's point of view, but by the last paragraph we have moved into Mrs. Blake's head ("She could feel his discomfort . . ."). The transition from one point of view to the other is gradual, with several paragraphs of dialogue between. Still, the readers have adjusted to being in Markey's head (they were in his head for most of the previous page), so the shift to Mrs. Blake's head is jarring even though it's not abrupt. Enough of these shifts and readers can lose their involvement in the story.

And yet there are writers who manage to move from head to head successfully. How? Consider the following, from Alice Hoffman's *Practical Magic*. Sally's sister Gillian has just arrived on the stoop after an absence of many years.

Antonia is one of Sally's daughters, and Jimmy is Gillian's lover:

> Gillian stops to take a good look at Sally.
>
> "I can't believe how much I've missed you."
>
> Gillian sounds as if she herself was surprised to discover this. She's sticking her fingernails into the palms of her hands, as if to wake herself from a bad dream. If she weren't desperate, she wouldn't be here, running to her big sister for help, when she spent her whole life trying to be as self-sufficient as a stone. Everyone else had families, and went east or west or just down the block for Easter or Thanksgiving, but not Gillian. She could always be counted on to take a holiday shift, and afterward she always found herself drawn to the best bar in town, where special hors d'oeuvres are set out for festive occasions, hard-boiled eggs tinted pale pink and aqua, or little turkey-and-cranberry burritos. One Thanksgiving Day Gillian went and got a tattoo on her wrist. It was a hot afternoon in Las Vegas, Nevada, and the sky was the color of a pie plate, and the fellow over at the tattoo parlor promised her it wouldn't hurt, but it did.
>
> "Everything is such a mess," Gillian admits.
>
> "Well, guess what?" Sally tells her sister. "I know you won't believe this, and I know you won't care, but I've actually got my own problems."
>
> The electricity bill, for instance, which has begun to reflect Antonia's increased use of the radio, which is

never for an instant turned off. The fact that Sally hasn't had a date in almost two years, not even with some cousin or friend of her next-door neighbor Linda Bennet, and can no longer think of love as a reality, or even as a possibility, however remote. For all the time they've been apart, living separate lives, Gillian has been doing as she pleased, fucking whomever she cares to and waking at noon. She hasn't had to sit up all night with little girls who have chicken pox, or negotiate curfews, or set her alarm for the proper hour because someone needs breakfast or a good talking to. Naturally Gillian looks great. She thinks the world revolves around her.

"Believe me. Your problems are nothing like mine. This time it's really bad, Sally."

Gillian's voice is getting smaller and smaller, but it's still the same voice that got Sally through that horrible year when she couldn't bring herself to speak. It's the voice that urged her on every Tuesday night, no matter what, with a fierce devotion, the kind you acquire only when you've shared the past.

"Okay." Sally sighs. "Let me have it."

Gillian takes a deep breath. "I've got Jimmy in the car." She comes closer, so she can whisper in Sally's ear. "The problem is . . ." This is a hard one, it really is. She has to just get it out and say it, whispered or not. "He's dead."

The reason this works better than the Markey example above or the *Lonesome Dove* example at the beginning of the chapter is that Hoffman maintains considerable narrative distance for much of the scene, even when in a character's head. The voice describing Gillian's lonely and dissolute life is as articulate and well organized as that describing Sally's suburban existence. Readers aren't moving from an intimate connection with one character to an intimate connection with another, as they do with McMurtry. It makes the jumps less jarring.

So when would you want to make these kinds of jumps? Well, not often, since at the very least it risks literary transparency. If you have an overriding dramatic mood for the scene that doesn't really belong to any of your characters, then you might want to try this approach. The key element in Hoffman's scene is the way the two sisters' lives collide at this moment, and for that to work, Hoffman needs to create a genuine sense of what each sister's life is truly like. She can't do this from a single point of view, since at this stage in the story each sister seriously misunderstands the other. She can't write brief, separate scenes from the two points of view, since that wouldn't let her build to the climax of Jimmy's body. She has to jump from head to head.

Remember, though, if you are tempted toward a similar literary effect, that Alice Hoffman is an expert. Earlier in the Markey scene than was quoted above, the writer wrote alternating paragraphs from the points of view of Mrs. Blake (in the shower) and of Markey (walking through her building's lobby and riding the elevator to her floor). The writer was using this crosscutting technique to build suspense about Markey's approach, a technique that might have worked well, except that the jumps back and forth created more confusion than tension.

Say you want to track the emotions of everyone involved in the scene, for instance. You might naturally gravitate toward writing interior monologue for everyone, as McMurtry did. Yet using interior monologue in this way can be just a whit away from telling. Besides, readers need some time to settle into a given emotional state, so when you move quickly from one passion-charged head to another, you're likely to leave them behind. They'll know what your various characters are feeling, but they won't have time to *feel* like any of the characters. And that kind of emotional connection is exactly what you're after. It's almost always more effective to stick with a single viewpoint character and let the other characters' emotions come out through their dialogue and action.

Consider this example, from pages submitted at a workshop. A group of men led by Elwood are relandscaping the yard of a movie mogul, Zoltan Diesel, without his knowledge. Harley, one of Elwood's men, is perched on a telephone pole outside of Diesel's estate to act as a lookout in case Diesel returns. Ford is an acquaintance of Diesel's who shows up unexpectedly.

"What's going on?" Harley switched the walkie-talkie back on.

Elwood leaned back on the belt that held him high in the tree and yelled to Ford above the noise of the saws. "Mister, I can't be responsible for your car, you leave it there. We got branches falling all over the place."

"Who's there?" Harley said over the walkie-talkie. "Elwood, what's going on?"

"If we scratch that car," Elwood said, "our insurance don't cover it."

"Typical Diesel performance," Ford said. "Total disregard of anybody else's time. Whatever's going on, he can solve it." Ford gave a final puzzled look, got into the car—opening the door this time—and pulled out.

"Jesus," said Bart, "why'd you take a chance of talking to him?"

"Because if he stayed here, sooner or later he'd recognize one of us," Elwood said. "And we wouldn't be able to get out if he did. The Beverly Hills cops are fast."

This is a well-written scene with clear character voices and vivid details, but the writer is trying to capture too many things at the same time: Harley's confusion, Elwood's self-assurance, Ford's disgust. In the process she has muddied the point of view and reduced the reader's involvement in the scene. (There are at least two point-of-view shifts—finding them is left as an exercise.)

But what if she had written:

Harley switched the walkie-talkie back on and slapped it to his ear. "What's going on?"

He could hear Elwood yelling above the noise of the saws. "Mister, I can't be responsible for your car, you leave it there. We got branches falling all over the place."

"Who's there?" Harley said. "Elwood, what's going on?"

Elwood leaned back on the belt and stared at Ford below him. "Mister, if we scratch that car, our insurance don't cover it."

"Typical Diesel performance," Ford yelled back. "Total disregard of anybody else's time. Whatever's going on, he can solve it."

He threw Elwood a final puzzled look, got into the car—opening the door this time—and pulled out.

"Jesus," Bart said once he was gone, "why'd you take a chance talking to him?"

"Because if he stayed here, sooner or later he'd recognize one of us," Elwood said. "And we wouldn't be able to get out if he did. The Beverly Hills cops are fast."

Here, there are only two points of view—Harley's (which includes only what he could hear through the walkie-talkie) and Elwood's (which includes only what he would see and hear from the top of the tree). Because the scene isn't trying to do everything at once, the two dominant emotions—Harley's nervousness and Elwood's self-confidence—come through much more clearly.

It's worth noting that, because the emotional connection between your readers and your viewpoint character builds slowly, it's usually a good idea to establish the point of view as quickly as possible—in the first sentence of the scene if you can manage it:

"Everything was in place for a perfect day. Mortimer lay stretched out in the hammock, a novel propped open on his chest, lemonade on the lawn beside him, hat pulled over his eyes."

"Blanche stared at the rows upon rows of identical cubicles that made up her office and decided to pack it in and move to Montana."

"When she heard the first shots, Letitia was in the sitting room."

When you make the point of view clear at the beginning of a scene, you get your readers involved right away and let them get used to inhabiting your viewpoint character's head.

So what happens when you have to shift your point of view for sake of the plot? If, say, you are writing from Inspector Hendircks's point of view and want to establish that Farnsworth the butler is nervous, without letting Hendircks know—how do you change the point of view without jerking your readers around? It's quite simple: end the current scene, insert a linespace, and start a new scene from the point of view you need, just as we did above with the Harley-Elwood example. Linespaces prepare readers for a shift (in time, place, or point of view), so the change in point of view won't catch them by surprise.

For instance, take a look at this example from *Touch*, by Elmore Leonard. Lynn is being interviewed by Howard, a pushy talk-show host. Juvenal is watching from offstage:

"Hey, it's beautiful," Howard said. "You're young, you're in love. Heck, then what's wrong with sleeping together?" He paused. "Unless you're ashamed to admit it, feel it's something dirty, obscene." Howard frowned. "If you're in love, why should you feel guilty about sleeping together?"

"I *don't* feel guilty. I haven't said anything about . . . our relationship." The son of a bitch, he was even worse than she thought.

"You haven't denied anything either. Hey, I'm not judging. If you're having an affair with him, that's your business—"

"—but if you bring it on my show then it becomes *my* business because, honey, I can talk to you about anything I want—" Juvenal heard Howard say, as he was trying to hear what August was telling him through his clenched teeth, painfully, with great effort.

Here Leonard actually breaks the scene and shifts the point of view with a linespace in the middle of a line of dialogue, yet the shift is perfectly clear, and the sharp break adds to the tension of an already tense scene.

Once you have mastered your control of narrative distance, you can use it for some stunning effects. We once had a client who used varying narrative distance to build the tension in a scene in which a woman discovers her husband's body when she returns home from work. He describes the end of her commute—parking the car in the garage, walking up the sidewalk—with appreciable narrative distance. But as she gets closer to the bedroom where the body is, the client begins to use the woman's language and to allow her emotions to color the descriptions more and more, drawing readers further and further into her head, until the shocking moment when she turns on the light and sees her husband hanging from the ceiling fixture. This added technique for building the scene is so subtle that most readers won't realize it's happening. Yet it increases the tension almost subliminally, giving the scene a powerful payoff.

You can also start out in omniscient narration and then ease into a specific third-person point of view, in effect the literary equivalent of a camera moving from a long shot to gradually close the distance from the actor. Consider these passages from *The Jesuit* by John Gallahue:

> One morning in 1931, in early June, the pious routine of the rector of a sleepy seminary in Maryland was spectacularly interrupted. A young priest from the office of the Apostolic Delegate in Washington, DC, personally delivered a sealed message from Rome to the Superior of the House. He did not wait for a reply; indeed, as he informed the rector of the seminary, he had no knowledge whatsoever of the contents. Saying no more, the priest departed, leaving Father Dillon to peruse the brief message.

Readers, too, read the message, which demands extraordinary treatment of a young scholastic named Ulanov, and then we enter Father Dillon's head and the narrative distance begins to close.

> Father Dillon read the telegram three or four times. Finally he delegated one of his seminarians to fetch his confidential house consultant—Father Sullivan, a former rector now eighty years old. Together, they tried to comprehend the import of this extraordinary communication.

Note that the writing at this point, while in the third person rather than omniscient, is still fairly distant. Time is somewhat compressed, and the language is certainly not tinged with emotion. But by the time the two men have discussed the appointment, the language is more clearly Dillon's and there is a touch of edginess creeping in:

> The rector was still left with his power of decision, and he meant to exercise it. It wasn't that he found anything bad in the young man. No, that would represent a loss of balance, and if there was one virtue the rector prided himself on possessing, it was perspective. He simply sensed in the young Jesuit an empty spot. But even that wouldn't have mattered much if Rome hadn't been so insistent on his promotion.

Of all the means available to you for crafting your story, point of view is one of your most fundamental. It is how you show who your characters are. It allows you to convey emotions that often can't be put across in any other way. It allows your readers to share a character's concerns, to see, if only for an instant, the world the way he or she sees it. Indeed, along with dialogue and interior monologue, it is the place where your character's emotions belong.

Point of view is a powerful tool. Master it.

Checklist

- Which point of view are you using and why? If you want continuing intimacy, are you using the first person? If you want distance, are you using third person, or omniscient?
- Do you move from head to head? If so, why? Would your story gain power if you stuck with a single viewpoint character or broke your scenes up at appropriate places with linespaces to make this possible?
- Take a look at your language. Is it right for your viewpoint character? If not, should it be?
- Look at your descriptions. Can you tell how your viewpoint character feels about what you're describing?

Exercises

Spot the point of view problems:

A.   Susan heard the key in the lock box and then a second key in the front door. She grabbed Ed by the arm.

"My God, I forgot, it's the realtors."

He looked around the living room, at the papers strewn on the couch, the mail piled on the coffee table. He remembered the two days' worth of dishes in the kitchen sink. "What, you mean today? Now? With people?"

They had no time to lose. "You take the kitchen, I'll handle here."

Susan began gathering papers and shoving them in the fireplace, while Ed made a dash for the kitchen. Once there, he grabbed the dishpan and began stacking things in it as quietly as he could. He then hoisted the overflowing pan out of the sink and kicked open the cupboard.

No, they would look in the cupboard. Where then, the refrigerator? Behind the furnace in the basement?

He ducked out the back door just as Susan backed into the kitchen in front of the realtor and an earnest young couple.

"You're sure you wouldn't like to tour the upstairs first?" she asked.

"No, actually I'd like to see the basement," the young man said. "I'm thinking of setting up a shop in my home, and I need to know if there's enough space."

"Oh, very well."

Ed came back through the living room just as the couple disappeared down the steps.

"Okay, where are the dishes?" Susan said.

"Trunk of the car."

B.   A battered New York cab pulled over to the curb and Lance climbed in. The cabbie was a slight, withdrawn man who wasn't much given to conversation. This was fine with Lance, who buried himself in the *Times* as the cab wound its way north through the traffic choking the Park Avenue tunnel.

Finally the cab pulled up to Grand Central Terminal. Lance handed the cabbie a ten and disappeared into the crowd.

C.   *Take a sample scene of, say, an eight-year-old boy named Mitch in school on a Thursday afternoon at the moment he looks out the window and realizes that the first snowfall of the year has begun. Write this scene from the first person, third person, and omniscient points of view.*

Chapter 4

PROPORTION

Eammon flung the peavey to shore, reached down, and lifted Sunshine by grabbing his jacket collar with his left hand and his belt with his right hand. He then spun around, clutching the Indian's left shoulder, leaned down to put his right shoulder into Sunshine's belly, his right arm between the Indian's legs, and straightened up. He slowly turned on the log that was supporting them, moved down its length toward the bank, jumped to another log, walked the length of that one, then stepped on top of several logs running lengthwise of the river until he finally stepped down into the shallow water near shore.

On reading this passage taken from a workshop submission, it may well have occurred to you that it takes Eammon an awfully long time to make it to land. The Indian, Sunshine, has been hurt and the reader doesn't yet know how badly, and there's a great deal of action both before and after this point—the scene is an exciting one. But the writer undermines the excitement with his blow-by-blow (or log-by-log) account of how Eammon made his way to shore. The time spent on a relatively minor point has thrown the scene out of proportion.

Proportion problems like this one probably arise from the same lack of confidence that leads beginning writers to describe emotions they've already shown. It's hard to judge the effect your writing will have on your readers while you are writing it, so you tend to go overboard. While writing the passage quoted above, the writer presumably felt it was vital that his readers picture Eammon's journey over the logs precisely as he himself saw it.

And this sort of proportion problem has exactly the same effect on readers as excess description. When you fill in all the details and leave nothing to your readers' imaginations, you're patronizing them. This is even more true now than it was a few decades ago, when generous, detailed descriptions were the norm. It's the influence of movies and television again—readers are used to jump-cuts from scene to scene rather than long transitional shots. Fiction writers, in turn, are much freer to use ellipses, to leave more of the mundane, bridging action up to their readers' imaginations. For instance, instead of writing:

> The phone rang. Geraldine walked across the room and picked it up. "Hello," she said.

A writer nowadays can simply write:

The phone rang.

"Hello," Geraldine said.

And leave the rest to the reader's imagination. And the writer of the example at the beginning of this chapter needed only to write:

> Eammon flung the peavey away, grabbed Sunshine
> by his jacket collar and belt, threw him over his
> shoulder, and made his way across the logs to shore.

Of course, there are other things that can throw your proportions off besides simple misjudgment. Sometimes proportion problems arise when a writer is writing about his or her pet interests or hobbies. We once worked on a thriller that involved a seventeen-year-old boy making his way across the country, living off the land as he went. The book was generally well written, and the writer—evidently something of a survivalist himself—was given to precise, detailed descriptions of survival techniques, such as the best way to lash yourself to a tree limb so you won't fall off while you sleep.

Admittedly these details created an atmosphere of authenticity and established the writer's authority as a survivalist. And, yes, one of the joys of reading comes when a writer takes you through some little back alley of life that you never knew existed. But when we reached the three pages on how to kill and field-dress a beaver, we decided the writer had gone too far.

Even in the nineteenth century, the age of the long attention span, Herman Melville created a lot of problems for the readers of *Moby-Dick* by including lengthy passages on the natural history of whales. It's easy to drop out of a work of fiction that has pages and pages of passages like the following:

Book II. (*Octavo*), Chapter I. (*Grampus*).—Though this fish, whose loud sonorous breathing, or rather blowing, has furnished a proverb to landsmen, is so well known a denizen of the deep, yet he is not popularly classed among whales. But possessing all the grand distinctive features of the leviathan, most naturalists have recognized him for one. He is of moderate octavo size, varying from fifteen to twenty-five feet in length, and is as a general rule most stylishly dressed. He swims in herds, and has been seen in habitats as varied as the grand salons of the Lower East Side and the alehouses of Canarsie. Although an accomplished dancer, the Grampus is widely known as a poor conversationalist, and therefore should be avoided in most social situations.

You didn't read the whole paragraph, did you? If you didn't, you're not alone. The chapter on cetology in *Moby-Dick* may well be the least-read chapter in great American literature.

In a more recent example, Michael Crichton has drawn barbs on the proportion front, as in this excerpt from an otherwise favorable review by Christopher Lehman-Haupt of *Airframe* in *The New York Times*:

What Casey's team suspects may have caused Flight 545's problem is a "Slats deploy" with no autopilot override. The plane in question, an N-22, has had such a problem before. In case you don't understand what this means, Casey has been assigned an assistant who is ignorant of the airframe business to whom she says spontaneously: "You know anything about aerodynamics? No? Well, an aircraft flies because of the shape of the wing."

She goes on to explain: "When the aircraft is moving slower, during takeoff and landing, the wing needs greater curvature to maintain lift. So, at those times we increase the curvature, by extending sections in the front and back—flaps at the back, and slats at the leading edge." The trouble is, "if the slats extend, the plane may become unstable." And this appears to be what happened to Flight 545.

Casey will deliver such lectures at the drop of Mr. Crichton's fingers on his word processor.

Proportion problems can sometimes arise inadvertently, through cutting. That's what happened when Judith Searle's first novel, *Lovelife,* was put under contract at seven hundred pages during the era when editing at major houses wasn't so rare. Judith's editor made a number of suggestions for cuts. Soon the manuscript was trimmed to size. Gone were nearly all the cooking scenes, most of the philosophical and descriptive passages, and a fair amount of the interior monologue. Left intact were all the sex scenes. The result was a very steamy novel indeed, since the cuts radically

"Right about now the editors have reached the three pages on how to kill and field dress a beaver...."

changed the proportion of the sex scenes to the novel as a whole.

So how do you avoid proportion problems? In most cases, it's quite simple: pay attention.

Most larger proportion problems can be avoided if you pay attention to your story. After all, if you spend a great deal of time on a given character or plot element, for whatever reason, your readers naturally assume this element plays an important role in the story. So if the character you spend time on turns out to be insignificant or if you never follow up on the plot element you set up in such detail, readers are going to feel cheated.

In the first draft of a science fiction novel we edited, the writer devoted many pages to the nature of American society a century from now—developing along the way some penetrating insights into society as it is today. But after spending the first half of the book on this future society, the writer resolved the plot without involving that society at all. Instead, his hero simply straightened out some personal problems and then went on to live happily ever after. Since we expected the writer to use the society he'd spent so much time creating, we felt cheated by the conclusion, as if the book ended before it was over. In the next draft the writer gave more emphasis to his character's personal problems earlier in the book and then involved the futuristic society in his ending. The result was a much more satisfying story.

A warning: paying attention to your story doesn't mean ruthlessly cutting everything that doesn't immediately advance your plot. Anyone who's read one of P. D. James's Adam Dalgleish mysteries can tell you that atmosphere is an important element, even if its impact on the plot is often subtle. *Devices and Desires* takes us on a long tour through both the English countryside and Dalgleish's past relationship with his aunt before we see the first corpse. And some readers may well be bored by the slow buildup. But for most, a subtle tension runs through the buildup that serves to characterize Dalgleish most effectively, and the discovery of the first body has all the more impact because of it.

Properly proportioned does not mean textureless. There is always room for philosophical asides that reveal the narrator's character, subplots that may resonate with the main plot, forays into odd corners of background that make the fictional world more three-dimensional. The trick is telling the difference between digressions that harmonize with the story (even in odd and mysterious ways) and those that hang on the story like limpets.

One technique for telling the difference is to approach your work as if you were reading it for the first time. This isn't easy to do, of course—which is why editors come in so handy—but you can gain some objectivity if you walk away from your writing for a few days or weeks. When you come back, print out a scene or chapter and read it over. The idea is to react to the scene like a reader, not a writer, so you'll get better results if you read hard copy rather than on-screen. That way you don't have the temptation to fiddle with the text as you read. Instead, you can ask yourself what interests you the most, what really comes to life, what involves and intrigues. What moves or fascinates or disturbs or pleases you? Note your reactions in the margins or on Post-it slips. Don't analyze your reactions—you'll miss the subtle and mysteriously resonating stuff. And don't make any changes. Yet.

Once you've figured out what you like, take a look at what's left. Is it really needed? Does it add? (It can add without being needed in an obvious way.) Should it be shorter? Longer? This simple process can be surprisingly effective, because what interests you the most is very often what's going to be of most interest to your readers. If you feel uncomfortable with the number of observations made by a character, then your reader's reaction is likely to be at least as negative as yours.

And be prepared for surprises. If most of what you enjoyed doesn't obviously advance your plot, then maybe you need to change your plot. Clearly you're trying to write a story around the elements that grab you the least, and that's not going to work. It's far better to rewrite your story in a way that makes use of the good stuff than to simply to use your story as an excuse for writing the good stuff. In the end, you want to be able to cut most of what doesn't interest you and still have an intact, flowing plot made up of the stuff that does.

This method may not work when your proportions are off because you're writing about your pet interests. It's easy to convince yourself that those long passages on eighteenth-century theosophy, hand-cranking homemade ice cream, or the varieties of wildflower in a Blue Ridge Mountain meadow are vital to the texture of the story. And they may be. But bear in mind that most readers may not find such topics as interesting as you do.

Once you have trained yourself to see how changes in proportion affect your story, you can begin to use proportion to shape your readers' response to your plot. If you have some plot development that you want to come as a surprise, spend less space on it before you spring it on your readers. Or you could spend as much or more space on similar plot elements to mask the really important one. Using proportion to control your readers' response is subtle and powerful because it lets you manipulate your readers without their knowing they're being manipulated.

Agatha Christie used this technique in her first Miss Marple novel, *Murder at the Vicarage*. In that story, Miss Marple was not yet known as a shrewd detective. She was simply one more doddering old woman in a village amply supplied with doddering old women. So it came as a satisfying surprise when she gently explained that there *was* such a thing as a Maxim silencer, and the sneeze that was heard some minutes before the murder was supposedly committed may have been the fatal shot. Had Christie devoted pages to Miss Marple's deductive powers (or even to developing her character more than that of the other old biddies), the effect would have been lost.

An early draft of Fran Dorf's *Flight* presented the writer with a proportion challenge. Two of the main characters in *Flight* are Alan, the son of the town doctor, and Ethan, the son of the local crazy lady. Ethan, convicted of pushing his girlfriend Lana off a cliff (she survived), has been out of prison for eight years. Eventually the reader learns that it wasn't crazy Ethan who pushed Lana off the cliff, it was Alan; and through most of the book Ethan and Lana lead Alan's brother through a discovery of the truth.

The proportion problem arose because Dorf had to develop Alan's character in considerable detail. He was her villain, and the plot pivoted on an understanding of his personality. But because she spent so much time on Alan, her readers were likely to assume that Alan must be up to something—and so to guess early on that he was the culprit.

Dorf solved this problem by having Ethan escape from prison at the beginning of the novel, rather than him having been released eight years earlier. She also added scenes in which an unidentified character (Ethan, of course) stalked Alan—which set up Alan as a potential victim and so gave her a logical reason to develop his character. In effect, she controlled the proportions of her plot in order to mislead her readers.

You can avoid smaller-scale proportion problems—such as in Eammon's trip to the shore that opened the chapter—by paying attention to your characters. When you're writing from an intimate point of view, your viewpoint character's interest at the moment should control the degree of detail you put into your description. If your hero is fleeing from a Weedwacker-wielding madman, you can show his panic by describing the passing scenery in the blurriest of details. If your heroine is fighting a Weedwacker-wielding madman, you can show her focused attention by describing the battle in precise detail. In fact, allowing your viewpoint character's interest of the moment to control your descriptive detail is another way of writing from an intimate point of view.

Once you allow your viewpoint character's interest to determine your proportions within a description—how much detail you use, which details you describe first—you can use this connection to subtly create a sense of who your characters are. Perhaps the best example of this we've seen came from a workshop submission describing a chance meeting between two women, strangers to one another, at a roadside café. At one point the narrator noticed that her companion "had eaten all of her french fries but left her little scoop of cottage cheese untouched." That observation tells you something about the woman who ate her fries first, but it also tells you something about the narrator. It takes a certain personality to notice a detail like that.

Consider this passage, from Lee Smith's *Black Mountain Breakdown:*

> At the edge of the back yards Crystal can see their neighborhood all stretched out along the road. Lights shine at the back of every house, in the kitchens where the women are finishing up. Sometimes the black shadow of a woman's head crosses a kitchen window for a minute then vanishes. Agnes's mamma's shadow stays firmly there in her lighted square. That's where their sink is, by the window. In the front rooms, the televisions are on and the men are watching TV or reading the paper, tired. But not at her house. Crystal knows what's happening there. And sometimes she wishes she lived in one of these other houses, where probably some of the men have gone to sleep already, stretched out in reclining chairs. The Varney Boys, Horn and Daris, who are older, have got a big light on in their driveway and they are out there working on a car. That's what they do all the time. Their yard is full of parts of cars. Still they are good boys. Horn was the quarterback last year at Black Rock High, and they are Eagle Scouts. Crystal would like to have the Varney boys for brothers, grease-stained and open and grinning all the time. Not

like her own: Jules, who is so old she doesn't even know him, he's just thin and furious when he's home, which is almost never now, off teaching in a college, in Sykes, plain ornery, her mother says.

It's clear that we're getting the details that interest Crystal, and matters that might otherwise be distractions—the location of the sink in Agnes's mother's house, the Varney boys in their driveway—engage because they are grounded in her personality.

Once again, though, be careful when you're writing about your pet interests. If, like most writers, you've shaped your main character after yourself, then your main character may be far more interested in the coinage of the emperor Aurelian or experimental jazz from the mid-sixties than any of your readers. Of course, watching someone explore something they love can often draw readers in so that they become interested themselves, but the safest approach is to make sure the material you're writing about helps advance either your plot or your narrator's character.

Like so many of the other elements of fiction, proportion is a tool. If you use it without being aware of what it can do, you certainly won't use it to its full potential and may wind up doing damage to your story. But in skillful hands, it can subtly draw your readers into your story and bring it to life.

Checklist

- Take a look at your descriptions. Are the details you give the ones your viewpoint character would notice?
- Reread your first fifty pages, paying attention to what you spend your time on. Are the characters you develop most fully important to the ending? Do you use the locations you develop in detail later in the story? Do any of the characters play a surprising role in the ending? Could readers guess this from the amount of time you spend on them?
- Do you have tangents—little subplots or descriptions that don't advance the plot? If so, are all of them effective? If you don't have any, should you add some?
- Are you writing about your favorite topics or hobbies? If so, give careful consideration to how much time you spend on them.

Exercises

Correct the proportion in the following passages, both of which come from workshop submissions:

A.   As he approached the last hill, Carter passed two more runners who had started fast but were now spent and fading. They could no longer keep their arms up; their stride, once crisp and high-stepping, was now a tired, struggling, agonized shuffle. They licked their lips; their heads and shoulders drooped and swung desperately from side to side as if that extra motion could somehow coax additional reserve and speed from their aching legs.

B.   She walked to the sink, reaching for a glass and turning on the tap. "Watch out for the egg."

It was too late. Eddy [a four-year-old] was wiping his eyes and didn't see it. His foot slipped and he landed on the yolk. He began crying again.

Dotty wanted to cry. She grabbed Eddy by the arm, pulling him to his feet. Reaching for the dishrag, she tried to wipe his pants. "Stop crying," she said, handing him a glass of water. "Drink this, then go change your pants."

Chapter 5

DIALOGUE MECHANICS

Mr. [Robert] Ludlum has other peculiarities. For example, he hates the "he said" locution and avoids it as much as possible. Characters in *The Bourne Ultimatum* seldom "say" anything. Instead, they cry, interject, interrupt, muse, state, counter, conclude, mumble, whisper (Mr. Ludlum is great on whispers), intone, roar, exclaim, fume, explode, mutter. There is one especially unforgettable tautology: " 'I repeat,' repeated Alex."

The book may sell in the billions, but it's still junk.

—NEWGATE CALLENDER,
The New York Times Book Review

What's the first thing acquisitions editors look for when they begin reading a fiction submission? Several editors we know have answered that question the same way: "The first thing I do is find a scene with some dialogue. If the dialogue doesn't work, the manuscript gets bounced. If it's good, I start reading."

If you're like most writers, you probably find that writing dialogue takes more thought than writing narration or action. Your characters come alive—or fail to—when they speak, and it's no easy matter to put just the right words in their mouths.

And because it's such hard work, generations of writers have developed mechanical tricks to save them the trouble of writing dialogue that effectively conveys character and emotion—techniques to prop up shaky dialogue, or to paper over holes and make second-rate dialogue serviceable without a lot of effort. Not surprisingly, these are tricks to avoid if you want your dialogue to read like the work of a professional instead of an amateur or a hack.

Once you learn to spot these creaky mechanics, all you have to do is stop using them. And once you stop, you may find that your dialogue—standing on its own—is a lot stronger than you thought it was when you wrote it. (All those unnecessary supports you set up just make it *look* weak.) And should you find that your dialogue doesn't stand on its own, then at least you'll know where your next writing task lies.

Imagine you're at a play. It's the middle of the first act; you're getting really involved in the drama they're acting out. Suddenly the playwright runs out on the stage and yells, "Do you see what's happening here? Do you see how her coldness is behind his infidelity? Have you noticed the way his womanizing has undermined her confidence? Do you get it?"

You get it, of course, and you feel patronized. You're an intelligent theatergoer, and what's happening on the stage is clear enough. You don't need the writer to explain it to you.

This is exactly what happens when you explain your dialogue to your readers. Consider the following:

"You can't be serious," she said in astonishment.

If you're like most beginning novelists or short-story writers, you write sentences like these almost without thinking. What could be easier than simply to tell your readers how a character feels? If she is astonished, you just say so. It saves all sorts of time and trouble.

It's also lazy writing. When your dialogue is well written, describing your characters' emotions to your readers is just as patronizing as a playwright running onto the stage and explaining things to the audience. "You can't be serious," conveys astonishment—no explanation is needed. And when you explain dialogue that needs no explanation, you're writing down to your readers, a surefire way to turn them off. The theatergoer might or might not walk out of a theater when the playwright runs on stage; the reader who feels patronized is likely to close the book. Once again, Resist the Urge to Explain (R.U.E.).

And if your dialogue isn't well written—if it needs the explanation to convey the emotion—then the explanation really won't help. Say you'd written:

"I find that difficult to accept," she said in astonishment.

Here the explanation does let your readers know that your character is astonished. But you don't want them to know the fact, you want them to feel the emotion. You want your readers to be as astonished as she is, and the only way to do that is to have her say something your readers can imagine themselves saying when they're astonished. "I find that difficult to accept" doesn't quite do it.

If you tell your readers she is astonished when her dialogue doesn't *show* astonishment, then you've created an uncomfortable tension between your dialogue and your explanation. Your dialogue says one thing; your explanation, something slightly different. True, your readers probably won't notice—the truth is, only editors and reviewers really notice these things. But your readers will be aware, if only subconsciously, that something is wrong. And that awareness will undermine their involvement in the scene.

Think about it. There are as many different ways to be astonished (or angry or relieved or overjoyed) as there are people. The way we react under the influence of strong emotion is one of the things that makes us who we are. If you tell your readers your character is astonished, all they will know is that she is astonished. But if you show them how she is astonished through her dialogue or through a "beat" (a bit of physical action), they'll know a little more about her. ("She dropped the whisk, splattering meringue up the cupboard door. 'You can't be serious.'") It's showing and telling again, applied to dialogue.

"You can't be serious" also has a formality and coldness about it—compared to, say, "You've got to be kidding," or "You pulling my chain, dude?" A character likely to say, "You can't be serious," is also likely to be prim, proper, maybe a little uptight. And if all her dialogue conveys primness, then your readers will get to know her character without your ever having to use the word *prim*. Think of it this way: Every time you insert an explanation into dialogue, you're cheating your readers out of a little bit of one of your characters. Do it often enough, and none of your characters ever comes to life on the page.

Also, while most of your explanations will probably involve your characters' emotions, be on the lookout for those that explain the content of the dialogue:

> Percy burst into the zookeeper's office. Their callous mistreatment was killing the wombats and he wasn't going to stand for it.
>
> "Is something wrong, sir?" the zookeeper said.
>
> "Don't you realize you're killing those poor innocent creatures, you heartless fascist?" Percy yelled.

Again, if the dialogue already makes it clear, then you don't have to repeat it. Your readers will get it the first time. R.U.E.

Of course, dialogue explanations are rarely as obvious as that. More often they take the form of *-ly* adverbs, as in:

> "I'm afraid it's not going very well," he said grimly.
>
> "Keep scrubbing until you're finished," she said harshly.

"I don't know, I can't seem to work up the steam to
do any thing at all," he said listlessly.

Perhaps it's a lack of confidence on the writer's part, perhaps it's simple laziness, or perhaps it's a misguided attempt
to break up the monotony of using the unadorned *said* all
the time (more about that in a minute), but all too many fiction writers tend to pepper their dialogue with -*ly*'s. Which
is a good reason to cut virtually every one you write. *Ly*
adverbs almost always catch the writer in the act of explaining dialogue—smuggling emotions into speaker attributions
that belong in the dialogue itself. Again, if your dialogue
doesn't need the props, putting the props in will make it
seem weak even when it isn't.

There are a few exceptions to this principle, and almost all
of them are adverbs that actually modify the verb *said,* such
as "he said softly" or "she said clearly." After all, you don't say
something grimly in the same sense that you say something
softly. The grimness comes across more by *what* you say and
do—conveyed through word choice, body language, context—than by *how* you say it. Again, there are as many ways
to be grim as there are people, and when you write, "he said
grimly," what you are really saying is, "he said this, and he felt
pretty grim about it." You need to show the grimness, to show
what there is about your character that makes him seem grim.

Besides, if you use them often enough, -*ly* adverbs begin
to look like Tom Swifties—one-liners built around -*ly*
adverbs that are named for the archetypal example: " 'Hurry
up,' Tom said swiftly." Our favorite is, " 'Don't worry, the
radiation level isn't very high,' Tom said glowingly."

For a final word on the subject, here's a quote from an interview with Gabriel García Márquez:

> To tighten his own writing, [Márquez] has eliminated adverbs, which in Spanish all have the ending -*mente* [the equivalent of -*ly*]. "Before *Chronicle of a Death Foretold*," he says, "there are many. In *Chronicle*, I think there is one. After that, in *Love* there are none. In Spanish, the adverb -*mente* is a very easy solution. But when you want to use -*mente* and look for another form, it [the other form] always is better. It has become so natural to me that I don't even notice anymore."

Unless your dialogue consists entirely of one character talking to himself or herself, you will need to include speaker attributions so your readers know who is saying what. Bear in mind that the *only* reason you need them is so your readers know who is saying what. Don't use speaker attributions as a way of slipping in explanations of your dialogue ("he growled," "she snapped"). As with all other types of explanations, either they're unnecessary or they are necessary but shouldn't be ("Do you consider that amusing?" she whined).

Your best bet is to use the verb *said* almost without exception. ("I feel terrible about it," he said. "You always keep me waiting, you never call," she said.) Some writers get a little nervous when they see a long string of *said*'s spreading over the page. They hear the voices of their creative writing teachers telling them to strive for variety and originality in their verbs. So they write:

> "Give it to me," she demanded.
> "Here it is," he offered.
> "Is it loaded?" she inquired.

Or even worse:

> "I hate to admit that," he grimaced.
> "Come closer," she smiled.
> "So you've changed your mind," he chuckled.

To use verbs like these last three for speaker attributions is to brand yourself as an amateur—and to stick your character with an action that is physically impossible. No one outside of hack fiction has ever been able to grimace or smile or chuckle a sentence.

We're all in favor of choosing exactly the right verb for the action, but when you're writing speaker attributions the right verb is nearly always *said*. The reason those well-intentioned attempts at variety don't work is that verbs other than *said* tend to draw attention away from the dialogue. They jump out at the reader, make the reader aware, if only for a second, of the mechanics of writing. They draw attention to your technique, and a technique that distracts the reader is never a good idea. You want your readers to pay attention to your dialogue, not the means by which you get it to them.

"Nobody is going to be the least bit upset, Leonard, if you simply insert another string of 'saids'...."

Said, on the other hand, isn't even read the way other verbs are read. It is, and should be, an almost purely mechanical device—more like a punctuation mark than a verb. It's absolutely transparent, which makes it graceful and elegant. Which, actually, is another reason to avoid explanations and adverbs. Even when you use them with *said* (we said sternly), they tend to entangle your readers in your technique rather than leaving them free to concentrate on your dialogue.

There are other ways to keep your speaker attributions transparent. Don't open a paragraph of dialogue with the speaker attribution. Instead, start a paragraph with dialogue and place the speaker attribution at the first natural break in the first sentence. ("I disagree," he said. "Plungers have always been underrated as kitchen utensils.") This is an especially good idea when the paragraph is fairly long. The reader's ear seems to require the attribution near the beginning.

Place the character's name or pronoun first in a speaker attribution ("Dave said"). Reversing the two ("said Dave"), though often done, is less professional. It has a slightly old-fashioned, first-grade-reader flavor ("Run spot, run" said Jane). After all, "said he" fell out of favor sometime during the Taft administration.

Decide how you are going to refer to a character and stick with it for at least the length of the scene. Don't use "Hubert said" on one page, "Mr. Winchester said," on the next, and "the old man said" on the third. If you do, your readers will have to stop reading long enough to figure out that the old man is Hubert Winchester. Also, most people don't change the way they think of someone they're talking to in mid-conversation, so neither should your viewpoint character. This doesn't mean you have to stick with a single form of address for an entire novel, of course. If you want to show that your heroine is getting to know Mr. Winchester, for instance, you could have her refer to him as "Mr. Winchester" in chapter one, "Hubert" in chapter four, and "Hubie" in chapter ten.

If it's clear from the dialogue who is speaking—if two characters are bantering back and forth, for instance—you can dispense with speaker attributions altogether. But don't Ping-Pong direct address in an attempt to get rid of speaker attributions:

> "I just don't believe he'd say that, Chet."
> "Well, Hortense, I may have heard wrong, but—"
> "Cut it out, Chet. Just cut it out."

This technique may serve you well in a pinch, but it gets old very quickly. People just don't talk like that.

If you are still troubled by the number of *said*'s in your dialogue, you can replace some of them with beats:

> "I'd never thought of that before." Roger walked over to the fridge and helped himself to a soda. "But I suppose a good coat of shellac really would work just as well, wouldn't it?"

Remember, so long as your readers can tell who is speaking, your speaker attributions have done just what they need to do.

Substituting beats for speaker attributions can come in especially handy when your dialogue involves three or more speakers. In this case, you have to let your readers know who is saying each line of dialogue. But if the lines are brief, you can wind up with a string of *said*'s on the page that does get annoying after a while:

> "But didn't you promise . . ." Jessie said.
> "I did nothing of the sort," Tyrone said.
> "Now, look, you two—" Dudley said.
> "You stay out of this," Tyrone said.

If you substitute the occasional speaker attribution with a beat, you can break the monotony of the *said*'s before it begins to call attention to itself.

> "But didn't you promise . . ." Jessie said.
> "I did nothing of the sort," Tyrone said.
> Dudley stepped between them and held up his hands. "Now, look, you two—"
> Tyrone spun on him. "You stay out of this."

Don't get carried away with the technique. It's best to replace only a few of your speaker attributions with beats. A beat after every line of dialogue is even more distracting than too many speaker attributions. What you want is a comfortable balance.

One or two final mechanical points. First, use dashes rather than ellipses, as in the example above, to show an interruption. Ellipses are used, in fiction at least, to show a trailing off (as in the first line quoted above) or to show that there are gaps in the dialogue (as when you're giving one side of a telephone conversation).

And start a new paragraph whenever you have a new speaker. It will help your readers keep track of who's saying what. It's often a good idea to start a new paragraph for dialogue that follows a beat or bit of description, as in the "Dudley stepped between them . . ." in the example above. We'll return to frequent paragraphing later, but for now just keep in mind that good dialogue looks even better when you set it apart with its own paragraph.

But the very best thing you can do for good dialogue is never, ever to explain it.

Checklist

- First, check your dialogue for explanations. It may help to take a highlighter and mark every place where an emotion is mentioned outside of dialogue. Chances are, most of your highlights are explanations of one sort or another.
- Cut the explanations and see how the dialogue reads without them. Better? Worse? If it's worse, then start rewriting your dialogue.
- As long as you have your highlighter out, mark every -*ly* adverb. How many of them do you have? How

many of them are based on adjectives describing an emotion (*hysterically, angrily, morosely,* and so forth)? You can probably do without most of them, though perhaps not all.

- How about your speaker attributions? Any physical impossibilities ("he grimaced," "she snarled")? Any verbs other than *said*? Remember, though there are occasional exceptions, even innocuous verbs like *replied* or *answered* lack the unobtrusiveness of *said*.

- Can you get rid of some of your speaker attributions entirely? Just drop them and see if it's still clear who is speaking. Or try replacing some of them with beats.

- Have you started a paragraph with the speaker attribution?

- Name before the noun ("Renni said") rather than the other way around ("said Renni")?

- Have you referred to a character more than one way in the same scene?

- Ellipses for gaps, dashes for interruptions, right?

- How often have you paragraphed your dialogue? Try paragraphing a little more often and see how it reads.

Exercises

Try editing the following exchanges:

A.   "You aren't seriously thinking about putting that trash in your body, are you?" said a voice from behind me, archly.

   I put down the package of Twinkies and turned around. It was Fred McDermot, a passing acquaintance from work. "Pardon me," I said.

   "I said, you aren't going to put that stuff in your body, are you?" he repeated.

   "Fred, I fail to see how this is any of your business," I chuckled.

   "Paul, I'm just interested in your welfare, that's all," he replied. "Do you know what they put in those things?"

   "No, Fred."

   "Neither do I, Paul. That's the point."

B.   Gatsby *redux. This novel was Fitzgerald's masterpiece and deserves its status as a modern classic. But literary fashions have changed since* Gatsby *was published, and techniques that were perfectly fine then seem cumbersome today. So this is your chance to edit a master. Don't look back at chapter 1, and have fun.*

"I like to come," Lucille said. "I never care what I do, so I always have a good time. When I was here last, I tore my gown on a chair, and he asked me my name and address—within a week I got a package from Croirier's with a new evening gown in it."

"Did you keep it?" asked Jordan.

"Sure I did. I was going to wear it tonight, but it was too big in the bust and had to be altered. It was gas blue with lavender beads. Two hundred and sixty-five dollars."

"There's something funny about a fellow that'll do a thing like that," said the other girl eagerly. "He doesn't want any trouble with *any*body."

"Who doesn't?" I inquired.

"Gatsby. Somebody told me—"

The two girls and Jordan leaned together confidentially.

"Somebody told me they thought he killed a man."

A thrill passed over all of us. The three Mr. Mumbles bent forward and listened eagerly.

"I don't think it's so much *that*," argued Lucille skeptically; "it's more that he was a German spy during the war."

One of them nodded in confirmation.

"I heard that from a man who knew all about him, grew up with him in Germany," he assured us positively.

"Oh, no," said the first girl, "it couldn't be that,

because he was in the American army during the war." As our credulity switched back to her, she leaned forward with enthusiasm. "You look at him sometimes when he thinks nobody's looking at him. I'll bet he killed a man."

Chapter 6

SEE HOW IT SOUNDS

But it's when [the characters] start talking to one
another that their real problems begin.

After Lady Anne announces that she's got tickets for
the theater, her son gushes: " 'Macbeth'! Oh, Mummy,
I love you! It's the one I've always wanted to see." Later,
Sir Peter declares: "I'll never be free again. You killed
her, Greta. And then you made me part of what you'd
done. You and your psychopath." The psychopath in
question soon remarks: "Yeah, DNA. The scientists
have got the better of us . . . Just grab a blood sample,
send it off to the lab, and hey presto, Johnny Burglar
gets 10 years."

—GEOFF NICHOLSON, reviewing Simon Tolkien's
Final Witness in *The New York Times*

As Nicholson's review suggests, the problem with dialogue is, more often than not, with the dialogue itself rather

than with the mechanics. The creation of character voice—writing dialogue that reflects your characters' vocabularies, histories, and emotions—is one of your greatest challenges as a writer. Professional mechanics can make good dialogue dazzling, but what do you do if your dialogue is weak to begin with?

Contrary to popular wisdom, you *can* be taught to write better dialogue, but that subject would take a book of its own. In the meantime, there are some mechanical techniques you can use when self-editing that will cure one of the most common reasons for flat, voiceless dialogue: formality.

The difficulty is that all dialogue is formal to some extent. If dialogue were an accurate representation of the way most people actually talk most of the time, it would read like this:

> "Good morning," he said.
> "Good morning," she said.
> "How was the weekend?"
> "Oh, fine, fine. Got some stuff done."
> "Oh, yeah?"
> "Yeah, yeah. Cut the lawn, trimmed the hedges, you know, things like that."
> "Umm-humm."
> "How about yourself?"
> "Me? Uh, pretty much the same, I guess. Cut back the lilacs."
> "Yeah, the lilacs. Grow like weeds, don't they?"
> "Yeah."

If you were to write dialogue like this at novel length, your readers would nod off before they finished your first chapter. The dialogue you're trying to create has to be much more compressed, much more focused than real speech. In effect, dialogue is an artificial creation that sounds natural when you read it.

Most writers go overboard, creating dialogue so artificial that it becomes stilted and formal—again, it doesn't sound like anything anyone on this planet, in this century, would actually say. As a result, all the characters sound alike. Stilted speech is stilted speech no matter who speaks it.

The simplest way to make your dialogue less formal is to use more contractions. "I would not do that if I were you" sounds made up, where "I wouldn't do that if I were you" sounds like something a person would actually say. *You* use contractions, and so should your characters. And if you want to convey that a character is stiff—that he's pompous or his first language isn't English, or she's prissy—then dispensing with the contractions is an elegant way to go. "Is it not wonderful?" just has that continental flair.

Another helpful technique is to use sentence fragments. Consider this exchange:

> "Is she pregnant?"
> "It doesn't matter whether she is or not. She's not going to marry him."

It sounds much less formal—and more like real speech—if you edit it to read:

"Contrary to popular wisdom one can be taught to write better dialogue."

"Is she pregnant?"

"Doesn't matter whether she is or not, she's not going to marry him."

In the second exchange, the writer has used another technique (in addition to the sentence fragment) to good effect: the two sentences in the answer to the question are strung together with a comma instead of the (grammatically correct) period. If not overused, this technique captures the rhythms of real speech remarkably well.

If your dialogue seems formal, also check to make sure you aren't trying to shoehorn information into the dialogue that doesn't belong there. We've already suggested in chapter 2 that you be wary of disguising your exposition as dialogue, lest it make your characters speak out of character. It also tends to make dialogue stilted, as in:

> "Dear," she said, "I realize it seems unfair of me to tell you this now, after eleven years of marriage and three children, but I'm not the woman I've led you to believe."

Again, you don't want your characters to speak more fully formed thoughts than they normally would, just so you can get some information to your readers. This doesn't mean you should never use dialogue for exposition, of course. Dialogue can be an excellent means of putting facts across. Just make sure your characters have a reason for saying the lines you give them, and that the lines themselves are in character.

Another way to make your dialogue more natural is to weed out fancy polysyllabic words unless the use of them is right for the character. "Have you considered the consequences?" sounds like something you read in a book. "Have you thought about what might happen?" sounds like something somebody might actually say. So have your characters "think" rather than "conclude," "give up" rather than "surrender," and "get" rather than "retrieve." What you're going for is short words packed full of consonants rather than longer, vowel-heavy words.

Another technique for loosening up your dialogue—one well known to successful screenwriters—is misdirection. In formal dialogue, questions are always clearly understood and answers are complete and responsive. Real life is rarely that neat. Consider the difference between:

> "I don't know what you were thinking about, going into a place like that. Are you all right?"
> "I'm fine, I really am."

and

> "What did you think you were doing, going into a place like that?"
> "I'm all right. Really."

The first version is clear enough, but the bit of misdirection in the second version gives the dialogue a little extra snap.

So have your characters misunderstand one another once in a while. Have them answer the unspoken question rather than the one asked out loud. Have them talk at cross-purposes. Have them hedge. Disagree. Lie. It will go a long way toward making them sound human.

For a striking example, notice the way Armand studiously ignores the questions Richie asks in this passage from Elmore Leonard's *Killshot:*

> "Armand," Richie said, "you're not married, are you?"
>
> "No way."
>
> "You ever live with a woman? I mean outside your family?"
>
> "What's the point?"
>
> "Armand, lemme tell you something. You're always telling me something, now it's my turn. Okay, Armand." If he kept saying the name it would get easier. "You might have shot a woman or two in your line or work . . . Have you?"
>
> "Go on what you're gonna tell me."
>
> "Let's say you have. But shooting a woman and understanding a woman are two entirely different things, man."

Had Armand simply answered Richie's question or told Richie to shut up, the dialogue wouldn't have the subtle tension and sense of authenticity it does.

Take a look at the following passage of dialogue from a workshop submission:

> "I wasn't expecting you until tomorrow," Anne said.
>
> "I thought it would be a nice idea to drop in."
>
> "Stan, I just got in about five minutes ago. I'm

fixing myself something to eat and then I'm going to get some rest."

"So, what you're trying to tell me is that I'm not wanted. Right?"

"Yes."

If you simply read it silently, this passage probably seems fine. The mechanics are transparent, and Anne's exasperation with Stan is clear without being explained through speaker attributions. But try reading the example aloud. We did, and this is the result:

"I wasn't expecting you until tomorrow," Anne said.

"I just thought it would be nice to drop in, that's all."

"Stan, I just got in five minutes ago myself. All I want to do is fix something to eat and get some rest."

"Are you trying to tell me I'm not wanted?"

"You got it."

The changes we made were subtle, but if you read both examples aloud, you can see the difference they make. The second example reads more like real speech.

Again, good dialogue isn't an exact transcription of the way people talk but is more an artifice, a literary device that mimics real speech. This means that even the best dialogue is by nature slightly formal. And because most of the dialogue we read has this touch of formality, our eyes are trained to see slightly formal speech as normal. So if your dialogue is stiff or unnatural, your eye may pass right over the stiffness as you reread.

The answer of course is to bring your ear into play when you're editing yourself. After all, we're used to hearing relaxed, normal speech in real life. Much of the stiffness in a passage of dialogue that doesn't show up when you read your work silently (such as the "Yes" in the example above) will spring right out at you when you read out loud. You may find yourself making little changes as you read. If so, pay attention to these changes—your ear is telling you how your dialogue should sound. The eye can be fooled, but the ear knows.

In addition to helping you overcome stiffness, reading a passage aloud can help you find the rhythm of your dialogue. Speaker attributions, when to insert a beat, when to let the dialogue push ahead—all of this becomes clearer when you hear your dialogue being spoken.

Some writers find it helpful to have a friend read through their dialogue with them, as if it were a screenplay. Others read their dialogue into a tape recorder and then play it back—more of the stiffness shows up when they listen than when they read. However you decide to do it, reading your dialogue aloud will almost always lead you to changes that make it sound more natural.

Reading dialogue aloud can help you develop your characters' unique voices as well. Select a scene in which two or three characters speak, then go through it two or three times—reading aloud, in turn, all the lines spoken by a single character. As you read the first character's lines aloud, you may get a sense of his or her particular speech rhythms, vocabulary, conversational style (self-interruptive or self-contained, enthusiastic or rigid), speech mannerisms, and so forth. Then read the next character's lines aloud, and if the speech style is the same, you know you've got some rethinking to do. As always when reading aloud, be alert for any "mistake" or change you make in the process of reading. It may be an improvement.

Everything we've just said about dialogue applies to narration and description as well. Consider the following:

> It had been Carl's rather desperate willingness to put himself and his home on display for the membership committee that finally convinced me that something would have to be done about the longtime erosion of our marriage. The thought of joining such a group had never occurred to me, and I realized that Carl and I not only no longer thought the same way about things, we didn't even think about the same things.

Once again, the passage looks perfectly fine, but if you read it aloud, you will probably find yourself tripping over the wording from time to time—the "Carl and I not only no longer thought," for instance. As edited, the passage reads:

> Actually, it had been Carl's eagerness to put himself and his home (and his wife) on display for the membership committee that finally convinced me something specific would have to be done about the

longtime erosion of our marriage. The thought of joining such a group had never occurred to me. I realized then that not only did Carl and I no longer think the same way about things, we didn't even think about the same things.

Even writing that was never intended to be (and probably never will be) read aloud can be improved if you read aloud as you revise. Every word of this book was read aloud several times in the course of revision. Passages of narration and description will read better once they have the sense of rhythm and flow you edit in while (or after) reading them aloud.

A century ago, Mark Twain could write a novel full of passages like this one—

> "Why, Huck, doan' de French people talk de same way we does?"
>
> "*No,* Jim; you couldn't understand a word they said—not a single word."
>
> "Well, now, I be ding-busted! How do dat come?"
>
> "*I* don't know; but it's so. I got some of their jabber out a book. Spose a man was to come to you and say *Polly-voo-franzy*—what would you think?"
>
> "I wouldn' think nuff'n; I'd take en bust him over de head."

—and get away with it.

Times have changed, and few writers today would write dialogue as hard to follow as Twain's. But beginning novelists even today are often tempted to write dialect—whether it be southern black or Bronx Italian or Locust Valley lock-jaw—using a lot of trick spellings and lexical gimmicks. It's the easy way out.

And like most easy ways, it's not the best way. When you use an unusual spelling, you are bound to draw the reader's attention away from the dialogue and onto the means of getting it across. If the dialect gets thick enough, it isn't read so much as translated—as any modern reader of *Huckleberry Finn* can tell you. The occasional dialectical spelling won't get you into trouble with your readers, but it doesn't take much to make too much.

So how *do* you get a character's geographical or educational or social background across? The best way is through word choice, cadence, and grammar. If you can capture the particular rhythm, the music in, say, a New England Yankee's way of speaking, you'll have put your character across with great effectiveness.

Consider this example, taken from Ed McBain's review of *The Secret Pilgrim* by John le Carré:

> It comes as no surprise that le Carré's tone-perfect
> ear can recreate in English even the cadences and styles
> of people speaking in foreign tongues. Listen, for
> example, to the German girl Britta, a prisoner of the
> Israelis, talking to Ned in her native tongue, transcribed
> as English:
> "Are you inadequate, Mr. Nobody? I think perhaps
> you are. In your occupation, that is normal. You should
> join us, Mr. Nobody. You should take lessons with us,

and we shall convert you to our cause. Then you will be adequate."

Isn't that German we're reading?

And then there is the following example, from Catherine Cottle's *The Price of Milk and Honey:*

"I didn't stay up to fight," she said. "But I got to find out what it is keeping us here. What it is keeping my children from being somebody."

"They already be somebody. They *born* somebodies."

"Somebody to do what? Work the cane field? All I want is what's good for us and the children."

"You making me crazy, that's what you doing. I used to could forget about the cane field at night. I used to not remember about my papa and my mama so much. Now—"

"If we left here, you wouldn't see the cane field no more. You wouldn't have nightmares about your papa and your mama, neither. I can't understand why you stay."

"Why I got to give you a reason? Reason ain't no pain killer. Reason ain't no free-feeling good world."

Notice that the writer never changes a spelling, never even drops a *g*. There are no explanations, no adverbs, and no speaker attributions beyond the first one. There is one interruption, one bit of misdirection, and neither of the characters speaks more than three sentences in a row.

But read the passage aloud. When you do, you can feel how right the words are, how well they fit the mouths of the writer's southern black characters. It takes courage to write a line like, "Reason ain't no free-feeling good world." But the results are worth the risk. You can imagine real, live people saying these words.

That's what you should strive for in all your dialogue— to give a sense that the words you write are words real people would actually speak. Explanations, *-ly* adverbs, oddball verbs of speech, trick spellings—these can't really help your dialogue because they don't really change the dialogue. They take the place of good dialogue rather than help create it.

And if you're serious about writing fiction well, you will accept no substitutes.

Checklist

- First, read your dialogue aloud. Read your narration out loud, for that matter. At some point or another, you should read aloud every word you write.
- As you read, be on the lookout for places where you are tempted to change the wording. Give in to this temptation whenever you can.
- How smooth and polished is your dialogue? Could you use more contractions, more sentence fragments, more run-on sentences?
- Is your stiff dialogue really exposition in disguise?

- How well do your characters understand one another? Do they ever mislead one another? Any outright lies?
- How about dialect? Are you using a lot of unusual spellings and other lexical tricks? If you rewrite your dialect with standard spellings, does it still read like dialect?

Exercises

A.   *This exercise was taken from one of our workshop submissions. Try to edit it so as to get rid of some of the formality.*

As they sat quietly catching their breath, Getz said, "We've all been diving together for a long time and are very comfortable with each other. I understand you're experienced but you are new to us, so I wonder if you would mind my giving you a quick quiz, just to satisfy ourselves of your basic competence?"

"Go ahead, sir."

"Okay, this is easy. What is your maximum no-decompress bottom time at three atmospheres?"

"The U.S. Navy tables allow sixty minutes at sixty feet with a standard rate of ascent."

"Good work, Mr. Wheeler. Welcome aboard. You see, we try not to take chances. We are frequently more than ten hours from a competent physician and there is no recompression chamber in the country. We don't 'push the tables.' "

Lou grinned boyishly, speaking with a cigarette in his mouth. "You mean we don't *regularly* 'push the tables.' "

B.   *The following passage was originally written by one of the writers of this book as a workshop exercise. Be forewarned, it includes every dialogue point we've made in the last two chapters, and a few points we will make in chapters yet to come.*

I peered through the front window of the garage, which did me no good, since light hadn't been able to penetrate that window since man walked on the moon. "Anybody here?" I tapped on the door.

A man came out from the shop wearing greasy, half-unzipped coveralls with the name "Lester" stitched over the pocket. I hoped he took those off before he got into my car.

"Yeah, wha' can I do for youse?" he grumbled as he took his cigar stub out of his mouth and spat near my feet.

"Well, my name is Mr. Baumgarten. I'm here to pick up my car. Is it ready?" I said sweetly. Truth is, I was ready to get the car away from him whether it was ready or not.

"Hang onna sec." He stepped back into the

shop and picked up a greasy clipboard with a thick wad of forms under the clip. "Wha' wuzza name again, Bumgarden?"

"BAUMgarten," I said. You cretin, I thought.

"Yeah, right," he said, pawing through the forms. "Don't see youse here, Mr. BAUMgarden. Sorry."

"What do you mean, sorry? You have my car in there. Either it's fixed or it's not." I'm a patient man, but my blood was beginning to boil.

"Loo', mistah, whaddya think—I got time to get, like, intimit wid all my clientele?" Oh, I bet you get intimate if they're pretty enough, I thought. "You could be BAUMgarden, you could be his cousin, you could be Governor Pataki for all I know," he went on. "But I ain't givin you no car 'less you got papers and I got matchin' papers. Far as I'm concerned, you ain't on this clipboard, you don't exist."

Chapter 7

INTERIOR MONOLOGUE

Big Jim Billups fondled the .38 in his pocket, waddled over to the back of his truck, and spat. Could've stopped the whole damn thing last night—they didn't carry no guns. What was the use of doing a job if you didn't do a good one? He rocked, shifting his weight from one leg to another, and spat again. The sound of the marchers was closer now.

Soon it would be time.

So far we've looked at two places where you can put the character emotion you've stripped out of your dialogue mechanics—into the dialogue itself and into the language of your descriptions written from an intimate point of view. A third place is interior monologue. Movies and television may be influencing writers to write more visually, using immediate scenes with specific points of view to put their stories across. But fiction can always accomplish something that visual media will never be able to touch. If the passage above (taken from a workshop submission) were to be filmed, a skillful actor such as Nick Nolte could show that Big Jim is waiting for something, that he's nervous, and that he's a bit disgusted. But the viewers would never know exactly how he felt or why.

Yet on the page, readers can see how he feels because they have the opportunity to move from action to thought and back again without ever being aware that anything out of the ordinary is happening. And yet what's happening is, when you think about it, remarkable. We're being allowed to see the action going on inside Big Jim's head. One of the great gifts of literature is that it allows for the expression of unexpressed thoughts: interior monologue.

As you might expect, allowing your readers to see what your character is thinking is a powerful, intimate way to establish that character's personality. And, as you also might expect, interior monologue is so powerful and easy to write—though, not to write well—that many fiction writers tend to overuse it. Take a look at the passage that follows, taken from a workshop submission:

"Mike, why are you here?" She asked this in what she hoped sounded like a neutral and reasonable tone. She knew how close she was to losing her defenses and made a special effort to pull back and regard Mike with professional distance.

"I need your help," he said.

"Why come to me?" After all, he knew she hated him.

"Because I trust you."

Laura shook her head and pulled a note pad from the top drawer of her desk.

"I'll give you the names of three excellent therapists," she said, head buried in the paper, "and you can choose the one you feel most comfortable with."

"Not that kind of help." His voice was commanding and demanding simultaneously. "No, this is in the nature of police work."

Laura felt herself becoming angry at him and his intrusion into her life. The sooner he left the better. "Get to the point, Mike."

If you're like most readers, you found this passage a little irritating. Constant interruptions are just as annoying on the page as they are in life, and this writer has interrupted her dialogue with interior monologue over and over again. Just about every line is followed by an excursion into Laura's head.

So how do you know you've gone too far with interior monologue? Some of these monologues express thoughts that are already clear from the dialogue itself ("He knew she hated him"), and many of them are dialogue explanations in disguise ("Laura felt herself becoming angry"). But even if all of them were legitimate, insightful passages of interior monologue, there are so many that they interrupt the drive of the dialogue, which itself can express emotion.

It's also possible to have too little interior monologue. Consider the following scene from a client's submission, Nia, a prosecuting attorney, is back in her hometown for the first time in thirty years for the funeral of her father. Her policeman husband, Simon, has stayed behind to testify in a trial. Rupert is the DA and her boss.

I was in the shower when the telephone rang. I grabbed a towel and hurried back to the bedroom.

"Hey, baby," Simon said.

"Hi," I said.

"How're things going up there?"

"Aunt Celeste and I planned the funeral this morning. I also went to the hospital to visit Aunt Babe. She has heart problems."

"I wish I could be there with you, but it looks like I'm going to be on the stand longer than we thought. The defense attorney said this morning that his cross will last a couple of days."

"You and Rupert getting along?"

"Let's just say he's staying out of my way and I'm staying out of his."

"Whatever it takes."

"You know," he said, "I was thinking we should go away for a few days."

"I can't leave Beulahville that soon. I've got to settle Daddy's estate, sell the house—"

"There'll be plenty of time to do all of that when we get back."

"It's not a good time, Simon."

"Actually, I've already booked a condo in Nag's Head. My supervisor said it's a real nice beach."

"I thought you said you were just thinking about it."

"I did think about it and I made a decision. I was hoping you'd be happy."

"I'm sorry, but I can't go."

"You have to go. If you don't I'll lose my deposit."

"That's not my fault, Simon. You should've asked me about this before you made the reservation."

"I was trying to do something nice for you. I guess I shouldn't have bothered."

The dialogue is sharp and has nice character voice, and Simon's manipulation starts to become apparent by the end of the scene. But if you were to read this snippet of dialogue in isolation, you might think that Simon and Nia get along fairly well. Actually, the context shows that she's too exhausted to deal with his manipulation and feels imposed upon by the entire conversation. But her exhaustion and intimidation need to be present in the scene as well as in the context. She doesn't stop feeling these things while she is on the phone with him. Because she's too intimidated to confront him, the writer can't show her feelings through dialogue. It would be difficult to work Nia's specific feelings into emotionally weighted descriptions without breaking up the rhythm of the dialogue. Also, unlike the subtle emotions that are best conveyed through such weighted descriptions, her emotions are conscious. She knows she's exhausted and intimidated. The best solution for showing her feelings is interior monologue. So take another look at the passage with some interior monologue added:

I was in the shower when the telephone rang. I grabbed a towel and hurried back to the bedroom.

"Hey, baby," Simon said.

Damn. I wasn't sure I had the energy to deal with Celeste again, let alone Simon. But putting him off was just a shortcut to a scene, so all I said was, "Hi."

"How're things going up there?"

"Aunt Celeste and I planned the funeral this morning. I also went to the hospital to visit Aunt Babe. She has heart problems."

"I wish I could be there with you, but it looks like I'm going to be on the stand longer than we thought. The defense attorney said this morning that his cross will last a couple of days."

"You and Rupert getting along?"

"Let's just say he's staying out of my way and I'm staying out of his."

God, another worry. I could imagine the jury picking up on the tension, and if the DA doesn't like his own witness, why should they? But I couldn't deal with this right now, so all I said was, "Whatever it takes."

"You know," he said, "I was thinking we should go away for a few days."

"I can't leave Beulahville that soon," I said. "I've got to settle Daddy's estate, sell the house—"

"There'll be plenty of time to do all of that when we get back."

"It's not a good time, Simon."

"Actually, I've already booked a condo in Nag's Head. My supervisor said it's a real nice beach."

Double damn. I sagged into Daddy's old rump-sprung recliner. "I thought you said you were just thinking about it."

"I did think about it and I made a decision. I was hoping you'd be happy."

"I'm sorry, but I can't go."

"You have to go. If you don't I'll lose my deposit."

"That's not my fault, Simon. You should've asked me about this before you made the reservation."

"I was trying to do something nice for you. I guess I shouldn't have bothered."

So what's the right amount of interior monologue? Sorry, you're on your own with that one. The balance you hit depends on what your characters are feeling, how important their feelings are to the story at that point, how you want the scene to flow, and, especially, how evident their feelings are in other ways. But if you're aware of what interior monologue can accomplish, you're on your way to finding the balance that works for you.

Once you have, how do you handle your mechanics so that the interior monologue reads smoothly and professionally? As with dialogue mechanics, the sterling value is unobtrusiveness. And there is one actual rule, about the only one we will give you: Never, ever use quotes with your interior monologue. It is not merely poor style; it is, by today's standards, ungrammatical. Thoughts are thought, not spoken.

"So far all her dreams have not come true but she wants high romance and a baby while her husband wants to be, and is, a very successful broker, who takes graduate courses at night and wants no baby and at the same time she has more or less recovered from being in love with the well-digger who dug her well, which is good since he is married with three children and is a drug addict and an alcoholic and he claims he's dying, although there are no signs of this and she says once she finds an outlet for her unrequited love she will lose eighty-five pounds. I enjoyed that sentence."

Also, it's rarely a good idea to have your characters mumble to themselves or speak under their breath:

"Yes, sir, I'll get right on it, sir," he said, then muttered, "soon as I finish lunch."

It might occasionally be possible to get away with this, assuming a sufficiently sullen character in a lightweight story, but it's almost always going to come off as a contrivance.

Other than these two caveats, how you handle your interior monologue depends almost entirely on your narrative distance. Everybody thinks in his or her own words, so your characters' interior monologue is, like their dialogue, always in their voice. To the extent that your narrative is in a different voice, you need to set the interior monologue off, to indicate that it's separate.

When the distinction is sharp, you could use thinker attributions—phrases such as "he thought" or "she wondered." Like speaker attributions, these mechanical tags usually serve to let your readers know who is thinking what. Very nearly the only time you need them is when you're writing from an extremely distant point of view, as in the following passage from James Joyce's *Portrait of the Artist as a Young Man:*

> A girl stood before him in midstream, alone and
> still, gazing out to sea. She seemed like one whom
> magic had changed into the likeness of a strange and
> beautiful seabird. Her long slender bare legs were
> delicate as a crane's and pure save where an emerald
> trail of seaweed had fashioned itself as a sign upon the
> flesh. Her thighs, fuller and softhued as ivory, were
> bared almost to the hips where the white fringes of her
> drawers were like a feathering of soft white down. Her

slateblue skirts were kilted boldly about her waist and dovetailed behind her. Her bosom was as a bird's, soft and slight, slight and soft as the breast of some darkplumaged dove. But her long fair hair was girlish, girlish, and touched with the wonder of mortal beauty, her face.

She was alone and still, gazing out to sea; and when she felt his presence and the worship of his eyes her eyes turned to him in quiet sufferance of his gaze, without shame or wantonness. Long, long she suffered his gaze and then quietly withdrew her eyes from his and bent them towards the stream, gently stirring the water with her foot hither and thither. The first faint noise of gently moving water broke the silence, low and faint and whispering, faint as the bells of sleep; hither and thither, hither and thither: and a faint flame trembled on her cheek.

—Heavenly God! cried Stephen's soul, in an outburst of profane joy.

He turned away from her suddenly and set off across the strand. His cheeks were aflame; his body was aglow; his limbs were trembling. On and on and on and on he strode, far out over the sands, singing wildly to the sea, crying to greet the advent of the life that had cried to him.

Here Joyce needs to write in a radically different voice from the young Stephen's, since young Stephen (like most people) does not have the artistry to precisely capture the epiphany he is experiencing. Joyce uses the thinker attribution ("cried Stephen's soul") to signal the brief shift into Stephen's own voice.

Passages like this should be the rare exception. Whenever you're writing from a single point of view—as you will be ninety percent of the time—you can simply jettison thinker attributions. Your readers will know who's doing the thinking.

> Had he meant to kill her? Not likely, he thought.
> Had he meant to kill her? Not likely.

Another technique for setting off interior monologue sharply is to write it in the first person (often in italics) when your narrative is in the third, a technique that is most effective when the passage of interior monologue is a self-conscious, internal thought—interior dialogue, in effect.

> He had just pulled his mail out of the box and was unlocking the door when he heard the metallic snap. He glanced back in time to see the Jag starting to roll slowly down the driveway.
>
> He broke into a sprint. The car was moving more quickly than it seemed to be, but he managed to catch up to it and grab the back bumper.
>
> *Great, what do I do now?*
>
> He stopped, panting, and simply watched the car sail off the retaining wall at the driveway's bottom.

Effective as this technique can be in letting readers into your characters' heads, be careful not to use it too often.

Interior dialogue can easily become a gimmick, and if over-used it can make your characters seem as if they have multiple-personality disorder.

Also, unless you are deliberately writing with narrative distance, there is no reason to cast your interior monologue in the first person. After all, if your interior monologue is in first person and your narrative is in third, it naturally creates a sense that the narrator and the thinker are not the same. If they are—if you are using the same voice for narrative and for interior monologue—your readers will have a subtle, almost subliminal sense of something wrong that could drive them right out of the story. It's far easier simply to cast the interior monologue into the third person, dispensing with any thinker attributions along the way.

Had I meant to kill her? he thought.
Had he meant to kill her?

And whether or not you are writing with narrative distance, it's not a good idea to cast all of your interior monologue in italics. Since long passages in italics (or, indeed, any unusual typeface) are a pain to read, you can only use this technique effectively for passages no longer than a short sentence or two. Even this brief passage is too long, don't you think? Also, since generations of hacks have used italics to punch up otherwise weak dialogue ("I have just about *had* it up to *here* with your get-rich-quick schemes!"), frequent italics have come to signal weak writ-ing. So you should *never* resort to them unless they are the *only* practical choice, as with the kind of self-conscious *internal* dialogue shown above or an *occasional* emphasis. Unless you really *need* italics they're just plain *irritating, aren't they?!!!*

Where you have a longer passage of interior monologue and are still writing with some narrative distance, it sometimes helps to set it off in its own paragraph, especially when the passage signals a change of mood:

> Monroe settled into one of the plastic chairs outside the examining room and flipped through a magazine.
>
> Who was he kidding, he knew he couldn't read anything in the state he was in. Still, better to look at the pictures in the ads than to stare at the other patients. Or worse yet, to think about what was going to happen.

But if italics, first person, or separate paragraphs are to be used rarely, what's the norm? How do you set off your interior monologue when you're writing with narrative intimacy? Quite simply, you don't. One of the signs that you are writing from an intimate point of view is that the line between your descriptions and your interior monologue begins to blur. Readers move effortlessly from seeing the world through your character's *eyes* to seeing the world through your character's *mind* and back again. Consider the following passage, from one of our workshop submissions:

> He flipped the book over and stared at the quote.
> "A masterpiece of clarity and insight by a leading

clinician and theoretician." The words were from
Jerome Carver, Jr., MD.

Pond hurled the book at the wall.

Jerry Carver was Pond's best friend, the one who'd
run off with Alice after Pond was released from prison.
Just when he'd needed them most. The attribution
should have read, Jerome Carver, Jr., Traitor.

The first two paragraphs of this passage are clearly
description, but with the third, the distinction becomes a bit
less obvious. The paragraph starts out with what looks like
backstory, yet by the time the paragraph is finished, it's clear
we're being let into Pond's mind. The interior monologue is
third person, past tense, and the language is such as Pond
would have used at the time if he had been speaking out
loud. The transition is so smooth the seams don't show.

And, of course, when you're writing in the first person,
you can achieve this sort of seamlessness almost automati-
cally. Note how easily we move from observations to
thoughts and back in the following passage from Sue
Grafton's *M Is for Murder*:

I surveyed the surrounding area. I spotted the folder
with all the newspaper articles about Guy's past
behavior, relieved that the cops hadn't swept through
and taken it. On the other hand, the search warrant
probably wasn't that broad. The list of property to be
seized might have been directed only toward the
murder weapon itself. I leafed through the clippings,
speed-reading for content, looking for the name

Outhwaite or anything close. There was nothing. I
checked through some of the stray folders on the desk,
but found nothing else that seemed relevant. One more
dead end, though the idea was sound—someone with a
grudge making Guy's life difficult. I pressed the file
under my arm and left the room, turning off the lights
as I went.

One final wrinkle. Even in the first person, there are rare
cases when you need to set interior monologue off from the
narrative voice. Some first-person novels are written with the
narrator looking back on events that took place in his or her
past, often because a more mature narrative voice can provide a worldly-wise perspective on the story. At times, it's
necessary for such a narrator to distinguish between what he
or she is thinking in the narrative present and what he or she
thought at the time of the story. Consider the following,
from Mary Renault's *The Praise Singer,* a historical novel set
in ancient Greece. In it the narrator, the lyric poet
Simonides, remembers from his retirement the time he was
invited by his brother Theas to return to his home city for
the first time after taking up his profession:

> Theas clapped me on the shoulder. "Next time,
> write a letter we can show off to our friends. No one
> knows you've become a scholar. But what got into you,
> not to know what to do? Have you been so long away,
> you've forgotten the Apollo festival?"
> It was true; I had. The moon was waxing now, and
> it came at the next new moon.

"Only stand up at the contest," he said, "and sing as
you did tonight, and the rest will be wondering why
they troubled to try."

It had long been out of my thoughts, to sing in
Keos. Time and change had touched the boy who had
flinched before; the roads of the earth and the ways of
men, learning and skill, pride and anger. A man
thought now, Yes, I could sing before my father.

Note that the description of his maturing over the years
("Time and change . . .") is written from the perspective of
the much older Simonides, who is narrating the book.
Because the narrative voice is much more mature than
Simonides's voice at the time, Renault has to use a thinker
attribution to distinguish between the two.

As we said earlier, gaining control of your narrative distance
can open the door for all sorts of effects, and this is even
more true when you work interior monologue into the mix.
Consider the following from a client's manuscript. Dr. Morris Fitzmaurice is a chemical researcher who has been sinking slowly into drug-crazed delirium. He is about to meet
with his board of directors to discuss his funding.

He entered the boardroom and discovered a reeling,
chaotic mess. All of the walls billowed with a hot,
demonic wind. The twelve members of the board had
taken on bestial aspects (or perhaps he was seeing them
for the first time as they truly were), and Morris

instantly perceived that the roast beef sandwiches they devoured as they waited for him in many ways symbolized their way of life—carnivorous, preying on the flesh of those weaker and slower. Jolas looked up at him with blood staining his teeth and smiled a smile that was more than fifty percent leer and Tinsdale reached out to take his hand as if to give one's hand in some way meant to acquiesce, to agree with the corrupt morals of these animals, to shake and in a sense wash one's hands of the slow rape of the environment which their kind endorsed, as they had since first a king declared himself to be better than those around him and raised around himself a noble class to aid him in living well off the sweat of others' brows just as these men had taken Morris's ideas and labor and bought themselves houses in Greenwich and Westport with tennis courts and pools, where their Negro servants came in to do their manual labor for them and they probably porked the maid while their wives were away and then when she had their illegitimate kid paid her to go live in Florida because she wasn't educated and didn't know she could get child support and she went along just like his grandfather had when these bastards came in and drove him off his farm his whole life and pushed him to drink and eventually killed him far younger than he should have died and now they sat smugly in their upholstered chairs and because they had money and power they expected Morris to suck the slime out from between their sweaty toes. Well, he wouldn't do it!

With his empty bottle of Cuervo Gold held aloft, the first words Morris spoke to the Board of Directors of Exeter Chemical were these:

"You filthy negro-maid-fuckers, you killed my grandfather. You bastards are going to burn in hell for the next thousand years. Your next twenty-three incarnations will be as cockroaches. Die, verminous scum."

That's the gist of how Dr. Morris Fitzmaurice lost his job at Exeter Chemical.

Note that the writer is making good use of a varying narrative distance. Most of the first part of this novel is written firmly from Morris's point of view, but as Morris gets crazier and crazier, the narrative viewpoint becomes more and more distant. The last three paragraphs of this excerpt are almost written from the omniscient point of view—which is fortunate, since a page or two inside Morris's head is all most readers can stand at this point.

We have noticed since the first edition of this book came out that a lot of writers have taken our advice about showing and telling too much to heart. The result has sometimes been sterile writing, consisting mostly of bare-bones descriptions and skeletal dialogue. Yet fiction allows for marvelous richness and depth, and nowhere more so than through interior monologue. You have to be careful not to go overboard, but interior monologue gives you the opportunity to invite your readers into your characters' minds, sometimes to stunning effect.

Mastering it is well worth the effort.

Checklist

- First, how much interior monologue do you have? You might want to take out the highlighter again and mark every passage that occurs inside someone's head.
- If you seem to have a lot, check to see whether some of your interior monologue is actually dialogue description in disguise. Are you using interior monologue to show things that should be told? Should some of your longer passages be turned into scenes?
- Do you have thinker attributions you should get rid of by recasting into third person, by setting the interior monologue off in its own paragraph or in italics, or by simply dropping the attribution?
- What sort of mechanics *are* you using? Are you using thinker attributions, italics, first person when your narrative is in the third person? If so, are you writing from a distant point of view? In other words, do your mechanics match your narrative distance?

Exercises

A. *Try your hand at editing the following:*

"Excuse me, miss, but I'm giving a seminar over in room 206 in a few minutes, and I need an overhead projector." The man at the door of the audiovisual room was actually wearing a tweed jacket with leather patches at the elbows. *All he needs is a pipe,* Kimberly thought.

"Okay, if you want an overhead or something like that—a movie projector or slides or whatever—you have to fill out a form ahead of time," she said briskly. "Then we can, like, line everything up and—"

"I know. I sent in the form three weeks ago."

Okay, she thought, that would have been when Ed was still in charge of AV. And he would have taken care of this, wouldn't he? I mean, Ed was a little sloppy and all—I'm going to have to clean up the office when I get a chance—but he basically got things done.

"You've been up to the seminar room?" she said.

"Yes," he replied, "and the projector wasn't there."

Oh, God, she thought. Great. I've only been in charge for fifteen minutes and already there's a major screw-up. "Okay, do you have your, whattya call it, your course form?"

He snapped his briefcase open, reached into it, and pulled out the familiar green card. "Right here."

Yeah, there it was, right on the form where it was supposed to be. "Give me a minute."

She ducked into the office and dug out the clipboard with all the requisitions on it. After five minutes, he got tired of waiting and stuck his head in the office.

"Miss? I don't want to be late," he said irritably.

"All right, mister." Jeez, she thought, he could at least give her a little time. "What's the course number?"

"A3205."

She went through the forms again. *Definitely no A3205 there.* "What's the room number?"

"As I believe I just told you, it's 206. I don't suppose you could just give me a projector now, could you? I'd be happy to carry it over myself."

"Nope, we don't have any to spare. If you want one, we have to figure out where yours went." She riffled through the forms one more time. Suddenly she found it. "Okay, here's the problem. I have room 206 listed as A9631, 'Making Fresh Baby Food at Home.' The projector should be up there."

"Miss, the projector's not there," he said dryly. "That's why I'm here."

Jeez, she wondered what it would take to please

this guy. "You're sure it's not there? Did you check the closet?"

"Room 206 doesn't have a closet."

"It most certainly does. It's the big seminar room off the cafeteria, right?"

"No, it's a smallish room near the elevators. How long have you worked here?"

"Long enough to know the building." *So there,* she thought. "Did you come across the courtyard to get here?"

"Um, yes, I did."

Ha, she had him. "Okay, we don't handle that wing of the building. You want the AV room for the Peebles annex; it's down by the bursar's office."

"Oh, I see." He looked at his watch. "Well, thank you."

"Hey, no sweat. We're here to serve."

B.   *Rewrite the following scene, changing the approach to that of interior monologue so as to create greater narrative intimacy:*

There had been no rain for two weeks. Last year's dried leaves crackled underfoot as Winston made his morning trek down Spruce Corner Road to the mailbox at the intersection. Then, just before he stepped out of the woodland and into the open land near Dymond's farm, he sniffed. Wood smoke.

Brush fire? It was too warm for anyone to be using

*a stove. Or had the neighbors started a brush burn
without a permit again?*

C. *Once again, you get to edit people who do this for
a living. These three writers all write immensely
effective interior monologue—which would be even
more effective with appropriate mechanics. So
have fun.*

"You see," Smiley explained, "our obsession
with virtue won't go away. Self-interest is so
limiting. So is expediency." He paused again, still
deep inside his own thoughts. "All I'm really
saying, I suppose, is that if the temptation to
humanity does assail you now and then, I hope
you won't take it as a weakness in yourselves, but
give it a fair hearing." The cufflinks, I thought, in
a flash of inspiration. George is remembering the
old man.

—JOHN LE CARRÉ, *The Secret Pilgrim*

"Did you go up there? When you were young?"
"I went to dances," the doctor said. "I
specialized in getting Cokes for people. I was
extremely good at getting Cokes passed around."
He helped her into a chair. "Now, then, what can I
do for you?"
Amanda sat her pocketbook down on the floor
and told him what she had come for.

Jesus Christ, he thought, wondering how many years he would have to practice medicine before he learned never to be surprised at anything.

—ELLEN GILCHRIST, *The Annunciation*

Dalgleish thought, This isn't my case and I can't stop him by force. But at least he could ensure that the direct path to the body lay undisturbed. Without another word he led the way and Mair followed. Why this insistence, he wondered, on seeing the body? To satisfy himself that she was, in fact, dead, the scientists' need to verify and confirm? Or was he trying to exorcise a horror he knew could be more terrible in imagination than in reality? Or was there, perhaps, a deeper compulsion, the need to pay her the tribute of standing over her body in the quietness and loneliness of the night before the police arrived with all the official paraphernalia of a murder investigation to violate forever the intimacies they had shared?

—P. D. JAMES, *A Taste for Death*

Chapter 8

EASY BEATS

"Laura's illness is very complex," I said. "If you'd just—"

"My wife obviously has a screw loose somewhere," he said. "I was under the impression that the family is informed when a person goes crazy."

I sighed. "Sometimes that's true," I admitted.

He said, "But you don't think my wife is crazy, or what?"

My frustration was mounting. "I wish you'd stop throwing that word around so casually," I snapped.

"I don't give a goddamn what you wish," he said. "It's obvious to me that my wife should be in an asylum."

What an odd choice of words, I thought. "There are no asylums any more, Mr. Wade," I pointed out.

He got up, walked over to the window and looked out, then turned back to me.

"Whatever," he said. "A hospital, then."

I took off my glasses, rubbed my eyes. "Why do you think she should be in a hospital?" I asked him.

"Delusions. You've heard of them?"

"Once or twice." I said sarcastically, beginning to lose it. "Why don't you tell me about Laura's?"

"Thinking things that are obviously ridiculous," he said. "Misinterpreting everyday events and people's behavior as having something to do with her—with this power she thinks she has. Oh, but I forgot. You believe in witches."

By now you will have spotted several problems with the dialogue in this example, taken from an early draft of Fran Dorf's *A Reasonable Madness*. There are some explanatory speaker attributions (and one needless thinker attribution), several dialogue descriptions, and one *-ly* adverb. Yet if you read the example carefully, you can see that underneath these mechanical problems lies some dialogue with real snap to it. The dialogue explanations mask the tension of the scene, but that tension is still there.

And yet, editing out the unnecessary dialogue mechanics is not enough to bring all the tension to the surface. Consider:

"Laura's illness is very complex," I said. "If you'd just—"

"My wife's obviously got a screw loose somewhere," he said. "I was under the impression that the family is informed when a person goes crazy."

I sighed. "Sometimes that's true."

"But you don't think my wife is crazy, or what?"

My frustration was mounting. "I wish you'd stop throwing that word around so casually."

"I don't give a goddamn what you wish. It's obvious to me my wife should be in an asylum."

What an odd choice of word. "There are no asylums any more, Mr. Wade."

He got up, walked over to the window and looked out, then turned back to me.

"Whatever," he said. "A hospital, then."

I took off my glasses, rubbed my eyes. "Why do you think she should be in a hospital?" I asked him.

"Delusions. You've heard of them?"

"Why don't you tell me what you think those are, Mr. Wade?"

"Thinking things that are obviously ridiculous," he said. "Misinterpreting everyday events and people's behavior as having something to do with her—with this power she has. Oh, but I forgot. You believe in witches."

The tension is mounting, yes, but it still falls short of the relentlessness it *could* have. Now take a look at the passage as finally edited:

"Laura's illness is very complex. If you'd—"

"My wife obviously has a screw loose somewhere," he said. "I was under the impression that the family is informed when a person goes crazy."

"Well, yes," I said, "but—"

"But you don't think my wife is crazy, or what?"

"I wish you'd stop throwing that word around."

"I don't give a goddamn what you wish. It's obvious to me that my wife belongs in an asylum."

An asylum?

"There are no asylums any more, Mr. Wade."

"A hospital, then. Whatever."

I took off my glasses, rubbed my eyes. "Why do you think Laura belongs in a hospital?"

"Delusions. You've heard of them?"

"Why don't you tell me what you think those are, Mr. Wade."

"Thinking things that are obviously ridiculous," he said. "Misinterpreting everyday events and people's behavior as having something to do with her—with this power she thinks she has. Oh, but I forgot. You believe in witches."

Now the tension is crackling. What's the difference? Self-editing for dialogue points helped, but what really improves the flow of the scene is the fact that in the second version the dialogue is interrupted less often. The revision contains fewer beats.

Beats?

Beats are the bits of action interspersed through a scene, such as a character walking to a window or removing his glasses and rubbing his eyes—the literary equivalent of what is known in the theater as "stage business." Usually they involve physical gestures, although a short passage of interior monologue can also be considered a sort of internal beat.

Beats serve a number of different purposes, such as allowing you to vary the pace of your dialogue. And as with interior monologue, it's very easy to interrupt your dialogue so often that you bring its pace to a halt. If good beats come easily to you, you'll be tempted to get carried away with the use of them. Or, you may be using beats to track your character's emotions, turning the beats into a running commentary on the dialogue.

Consider this example from Jill Robinson's *Dr. Rocksinger and the Age of Longing:*

> Hedy picked up some apples I'd glazed from the first bushel I'd bought. "You and apples." He put them back in the old bird's nest I kept them in. "Let's put on some music."
>
> I thought it might wake the children. But I decided not to mention that. I did sometimes play music when I was working. He saw me hesitate.
>
> "Are you worried about waking the kids? We don't have to."
>
> "Oh, they're used to it." I didn't say it was almost always Aaron Copland, the Best of Beethoven, and Mozart's Greatest Hits, and they would sometimes call down to me to turn it lower. I took off my jacket. If one was to be the seductive older woman one should probably not turn it down.
>
> He moved with authority through the records and tapes stacked by what I still referred to as the phonograph. "Why," Brynn always said, "do you think it's so cute to call it that? You know it's called a stereo. We don't want parents playing dumb."

"Bear in mind as you use beats to vary the rhythm, like a piece of fine music, your dialogue should have an ebb and flow to it.... Get your feet out of my face!.... You Rat-nosed Git!!....."

"Hey, this is nice." Hedy picked up a Chuck Mangione album I really did like.

"Oh, I adore that," I said. Something in common.

As with the Fran Dorf example at the beginning of the chapter, there is wonderful dialogue in here—surrounded by so many beats, both internal and external, that its effect is lost. The fact that the beats themselves are interesting and well written doesn't keep the constant interruption from irritating the reader.

Beats are also used to help tie your dialogue to your setting and characters. Beats provide those occasional little bits of imagery that guide your readers' imaginations. And, as with physical description, some writers may overuse beats because they lack confidence. After all, if you show every move your character makes, your readers are bound to be able to picture the action you describe. As in the following example from one of the authors:

> "Dad, have you seen the tickets to the concert tonight?"
>
> Nancy caught me in the middle of doing the dinner dishes, one of my favorite times of day. There's something soothing in the slosh of the water, the smell of detergent, the shine of the freshly washed plates. It's why I've never bought us a dishwasher.
>
> "Weren't they behind the toaster?" I scoured off a cookie sheet, ran it under the tap, and set it in the drying rack.
>
> She grabbed the toaster and held it up, spraying bread crumbs on the counter. "Nope."
>
> I sponged off a handful of butter knives, scraping a moment at a stubborn bit of crust. "Well, at the risk of sounding like a parent, where did you see them last?"

"I don't know, that's why I'm asking."

I rinsed the knives, dropped them in the rack, and started on one of the plates. "I don't suppose you've asked your brother, have you?"

She stared at me a moment, then said, "I'll kill him, I swear," and was gone before I could tell her to kill him quietly.

When you describe every bit of action down to the last detail, you give your readers a clear picture of what's going on but you also limit their imagination—and if you supply enough detail, you'll alienate them in the process. Describing your action too precisely can be as condescending as describing your characters' emotions. Far better to give your readers some hints and then allow them to fill in the blanks for themselves. This pays your readers the compliment of assuming they're intelligent and imaginative, and in a dialogue scene, allows your dialogue to flow more naturally.

Of course, it is possible to err in the other direction and include too few beats. Page after page of uninterrupted dialogue can become disembodied and disorienting after a while, even if the dialogue is excellent. Consider this passage from Toni Morrison's *The Bluest Eye:*

"What they going to do about Della? Don't she have no people?"

"A sister's coming up from North Carolina to look after her. I expect she want to get aholt of Della's house."

"Oh, come on. That's an evil thought, if I ever
heard one."

"What you want to bet? Henry Washington said
that sister ain't seen Della in fifteen years."

"I kind of thought Henry would marry her one of
these days."

"That old woman?"

"Well, Henry ain't no chicken."

"No, but he ain't no buzzard, either."

"He ever been married to anybody?"

"No."

"How come? Somebody cut it off?"

"He's just picky."

"He ain't picky. You see anything around here you'd
marry?"

"Well . . . no."

"He's just sensible. A steady worker with quiet
ways. I hope it works out all right."

"It will. How much you charging?"

"Five dollars every two weeks."

"That's a big help to you."

"I'll say."

Quite simply, the scene isn't as good as its dialogue.
What's needed are a few beats to anchor it in reality. If you
look back, you'll see that the edited version of the Fran Dorf
example above still contains one beat ("I took off my glasses,
rubbed my eyes") and one snippet of interior monologue
("An asylum?"). As with narration or immediate scene, the
idea is to strike the right balance between dialogue and beats.

So what's the right balance? Once again, there are no hard-and-fast rules, but there are a couple of principles that can help you find the balance that best fits your story. Remember, beats allow your readers to picture your dialogue taking place. As with other forms of description, you want to give your readers enough detail to jump-start their imaginations and enough leeway for their imaginations to work. You want to define the action without overdefining it. If your dialogue is taking place over dinner, for instance, an occasional dropped fork or sip of wine are enough to keep the readers in the scene. You don't need a description of the meal from soup to nuts.

How many beats you need depends on the rhythm of your dialogue. Like a piece of good music, good dialogue has an ebb and flow to it. Where you want the tension high, as with the confrontation scene that opens this chapter, pare the beats down to a bare minimum. If you've just had two high-tension scenes in a row, let your readers relax a bit in the next one with some quiet conversation interspersed with pauses (signified by beats).

Notice how the beats in the following passage from Stephen King's *Dreamcatcher* give a feel for the pauses in the conversation:

> "Okay," he says. "So you came in . . ." His eyes move as if watching her come in. "And you went to the counter . . ." His eyes go there. "You asked, probably, 'Which aisle's the aspirin in?' Something like that."
> "Yes, I—"

"Only you got something, too." He can see it on the candy-rack, a bright yellow mark something like a handprint. "Snickers bar?"

"Mounds." Her brown eyes are wide. "How did you know that?"

"You got the candy, then you went up to get the aspirin . . ." He's looking up Aisle 2 now. "After that you paid and went out. . . . Let's go outside a minute. Seeya, Cathy."

Cathy only nods, looking at him with wide eyes.

Although there are a lot of beats, the effect isn't interruptive. The beats act as a counterpoint to the dialogue—though numerous, they aren't pointless.

One situation that almost always requires a beat is when your dialogue changes emotional direction—when your character drops a pretense, say, or has a sudden realization in the middle of a line. For instance:

"I might have expected something like that from an ignorant dolt like you. Oh, my God, I'm sorry, I never should have said that."

doesn't read as clearly as:

"I might have expected something like that from an ignorant dolt like you." Her hands flew to her mouth. "Oh, my God, I'm sorry, I never should have said that."

The best way to fine-tune the rhythm of your dialogue, of course, is to read it aloud. Listen for the pauses as you read, and if you find yourself pausing between two consecutive lines, consider inserting a beat at that point.

Knowing where to put your beats is not as important as knowing what beats to insert. Beats do more than control the rhythm of your dialogue. They are also a powerful way to convey your characters. Any good actor knows the importance of body language in projecting a character, and the same holds true in fiction. A few years ago, a *New York Times* review complimented a new mystery on the quality of its characterization and demonstrated that quality by quoting a beat. It was just a little bit of action, but it told us more about the character than lengthy description or narration would have: "He blew his nose on the sheet."

Or consider the following passage, from Barbara Kingsolver's *Animal Dreams*. It has only one beat, but it's a good one:

> "You don't have to talk about this," I said.
> "I don't ever talk about him. Sometimes I'll go a day or two without even thinking about him, and then I get scared I might forget he ever was."
> I laid a hand on his gearshift arm. "You want me to drive?"

That one simple bit of action dropped into the dialogue in exactly the right place makes the driver's sadness over his brother's death more real to us and at the same time conveys the narrator's compassion.

Beats can also be pointless, distracting, clichéd, or repetitive. Haven't you read scenes in which the characters are forever looking into each other's eyes, down at their hands, or out the window? You want to write beats that are as fresh, as unique, as your characters. No two people cross a room in the same way, and there are as many ways of showing, say, uneasiness as there are situations to make a character uneasy.

So where do you find good beats? Well, as Yogi Berra once said, "You can see an awful lot just by watching." Watch your friends. Notice what they do with their hands when they're bored, with their legs when they're relaxed, with their eyes when they're nervous. Watch old movies— Humphrey Bogart in particular used stage business very effectively. Watch yourself. Keep an eye open for those little movements that bring your personality to the surface, the gestures that reveal who you are or how you're feeling. If you collect enough of these little movements, your characters won't ever have to look at their hands again.

You can also see an awful lot just by reading. Start paying attention to beats as you read—the ones that make you wish you'd written them and all the ones that distract or irritate. As you do, you'll notice that good beats, as in this passage from Eudora Welty's story "The Wide Net," are unobtrusive:

> "I've lost Hazel, she's vanished, she went to drown herself."
> "Why that ain't like Hazel," said Virgil.

William Wallace reached out and shook him. "You heard me. Don't you know we have to drag the river?"

"Right this minute?"

"You ain't got nothing to do till spring."

"Let me go set foot inside the house and speak to my mother and tell her a story, and I'll come back."

"This will take the wide net," said William Wallace.

His eyebrows gathered, and he was talking to himself.

The beat in the passage that follows, from Frederick Buechner's novel *Treasure Hunt,* supplies the all-important factor of the narrator's reaction to the dialogue:

"Of course [Mr. Bebb] raised me from the dead in Knoxville, Tennessee, dear. That was many years ago and you know the story. He was forever telling me he should have saved himself the trouble. He said I never really lived the life he'd gotten back for me, just shoved . . . just shoved it up my you-know-what and sat on it. He said hurtful things for my own good. He was my Rock of Gibraltar, and when he went, it seemed like he took my faith with him."

It was like driving past an accident. I tried not to look at Brownie as he spoke, but most of the time I couldn't help myself.

A longer beat can turn up the tension by slowing the scene down at a critical moment, as in this scene from John le Carré's *The Russia House:*

"Don't know a K, don't know a Katya, don't know a Yekaterina," Barley said. "Never screwed one, never flirted with one, never proposed to one, never even married one. Never *met* one, far as I remember. Yes, I did."

They waited, I waited; and we would have waited all night and there would not have been the creak of a chair or the clearing of a throat while Barry ransacked his memory for a Katya.

"Old cow in Aurora," Barley resumed. "Tried to flog me some art prints of Russian painters. I didn't bite. Aunts would have blown their corks."

"Aurora?" Clive asked, **not knowing whether it was a city or a state agency.**

"Publishers."

"Do you remember her other name?"

Barley shook his head, his face still out of sight.

"Beard," he said. "Katya of the beard. Ninety in the shade."

A beat can also provide breathing space in an emotionally tense scene like this one from Ellen Gilchrist's *The Annunciation,* in which the father of a child given up for adoption tells the mother he has seen their daughter:

"You went to look for her, didn't you?" Amanda said. "Tell me straight, Guy. I know you did. I know damn well that's what you were doing there."

"Let's go to your house," he said. "I don't want to talk about this in the car."

"Then stop the car," Amanda said.

He pulled the car over to the curb and turned and took her hands. "She looks like you. She's all right. She's married."

"What else?" Amanda said. "Tell me. Tell it all to me. She's blind, isn't she? I know she's blind. I've always known she would be blind. I remember when she was born her eyes were stuck together. I remember them being stuck together."

"She sees as good as you or me. She does everything. She was playing tennis. She won. I went to the New Orleans Lawn Tennis Club and watched her play."

"Then what is it?" Amanda said. "Tell me what you aren't telling me. Why do you sound like this?"

Guy turned his eyes away and let his hands drop from her arms. "She's very pretty and very ladylike and she's married to a young lawyer. You were right about one thing. If you'd kept on living there you would have met her sooner or later. You probably passed her on the street a thousand times."

"She looks like me?"

"Yes, but with dark hair. She's quieter. Well, I don't know that. I didn't get to talk to her. I just watched her play tennis. I kept thinking she looked like Grandmomma might have when she was young."

"She won?"

"Of course," he said. "Of course she won."

In a powerful, poignant scene from Anne Tyler's *Dinner at the Homesick Restaurant*, the beats accomplish both purposes simultaneously—increased tension and breathing space:

> "And see what I was like at your age?" **She handed him the picture with the tam-o'shanter.**
>
> **He glanced over. He frowned.** He said, "Who did you say that was?"
>
> "Me."
>
> "No, it's not."
>
> "Yes, it is. Me at thirteen. Mother wrote the date on the back."
>
> "It's not!" he said. **His voice was unusually high; he sounded like a much younger child.** "It isn't! Look at it! Why, it's like . . . a concentration camp person, a victim, Anne Frank. It's terrible! It's so sad!"
>
> **Surprised, she turned the photo around and looked again.**
>
> "So what?" she asked, **and she held it out to him once more. He drew back sharply.**
>
> "It's somebody else," he told her. "Not you; you're always laughing and having fun. It's not you."
>
> "Oh, fine, it's not me, then," she said, **and she returned to the rest of the photos.**

For the sake of contrast, take a look at the same scene with the beats eliminated:

> "And see what I was like at your age?"
>
> He said, "Who did you say that was?"
>
> "Me."

"No, it's not."

"Yes, it is. Me at thirteen. Mother wrote the date on the back."

"It's not! It isn't! Look at it! Why, it's like . . . a concentration camp person, a victim, Anne Frank! It's terrible! It's so sad!"

"So what?"

"It's somebody else," he told her. "Not you; you're always laughing and having fun. It's not you."

"Oh, fine, it's not me, then," she said.

The scene is still moving—the dialogue effectively conveys what's going on and its importance, and it's easy to tell who is speaking. What's lost is a great deal of the resonance, the deepening of the emotional content. You need the beats for those.

Checklist

- How many beats do you have? (It may be time to get out the highlighters yet again and mark all your beats.) How often do you interrupt your dialogue?

- What are your beats describing? Familiar everyday actions, such as dialing a telephone or buying groceries? How often do you repeat a beat? Are your characters always looking out of windows or lighting cigarettes?

- Do your beats help illuminate your characters? Are they individual or general actions anyone might do under just about any circumstances?
- Do your beats fit the rhythm of your dialogue? Read it aloud and find out.

Exercises

A.   *First, try editing out beats that don't work.*

"You're sure it runs?" Mr. Dietz said.

I leaned against the fender. "It did last time I tried it."

"Yeah, well, when was that?" He peered through the back window.

I picked at some dirt under my fingernails. "Just last week. Here, listen." I pulled out the key, hopped in the front seat, inserted the key, drew the choke, popped it into neutral, and hit the starter. The engine ground a few times, caught, and then sputtered and died. I pumped the gas once or twice and tried again. This time it caught and began to purr.

"Well, I don't know. It sounds all right, but I don't like the looks of the body." He kicked the tire.

"Look, for three hundred dollars, what do you

want?" I pulled the hood release, stepped around to the front, and lifted the hood. "I mean, listen to that, it's running like a baby. You should get twenty thousand miles out of this with no trouble. At least twenty."

He peered into one of the wheel wells. "As long as one of the tires doesn't fall off on me."

I slammed the hood. "There's a spare in the trunk. Now what do you say?"

B.   *Now for one where you have to put the beats in.*

"Do you really think this is a smart move?" she said. "I mean, you don't know anybody in California."

"I'm pretty sure," he said. "After all, it's not as if I have a choice. You've got to go where the jobs are."

"What about the kids?"

"Honey, it's not like I'm going to be gone forever. I'll send for you as soon as I can."

"Yeah, but when will that be? Where are you going to stay, what are you going to do, how are you going to live there?"

"I'm taking the tent, and I can sleep in the car if need be. Besides, I'll find something within a week, I'll bet you."

"I . . . It's just that I'm scared."

"I know. So am I."

Chapter 9

BREAKING UP IS
EASY TO DO

Read through the following confrontation between a talk-show host and his guest:

> In the final few moments, Curtin had pulled
> what he probably considered his trump card, laying
> the blame for every problem in Vietnamese life on
> the war. (On the American war, long over, Bernie
> pointed out, not the decade of war afterward against
> Cambodia. And not, surely not, on the vast portion
> of the Vietnamese budget currently going into the
> military. "Somewhere between forty and fifty
> percent, isn't it?" Bernie had asked pleasantly. Pat
> Curtin had blinked.) "Is it," Bernie then asked, "that
> America should feel so guilty for Hanoi's every
> brutality, every rigidity, every mismanagement, that
> we will rush to follow diplomatic recognition with
> reparations and foreign aid and trade and investment

and—what else? Delegations of unpaid experts?
Planeloads of privileged college kids, eager to play at
work they know they can walk away from?" Curtin's
mouth had tightened and Bernie, a veteran debater,
had smelled the panic of a cornered animal. Time for
the kill.

Now read the passage as edited:

"Finally," Curtin said, "one must realize that the
vast majority of problems today all come back to the
war."

"The American war, you mean?" Bernie had said.

"Of course."

"Not the decade of war against Cambodia?"

"Well, that—"

"And surely not on the vast portion of the Viet-
namese budget currently going into the military.
Somewhere between forty and fifty percent, isn't it?"

"They have to spend—"

"Is it," Bernie said, "that America should feel so
guilty for Hanoi's every brutality, every rigidity, every
mismanagement, that we will rush to follow diplomatic
recognition with reparations and foreign aid and trade
and investment and—what else? Delegations of unpaid
experts? Planeloads of privileged college kids eager to
play at work they can walk away from?"

Curtin's mouth had tightened and Bernie, a veteran
debater, had smelled the panic of a cornered animal.

Time for the kill.

You probably noticed that the first version tells, where showing would be more effective—the writer narrates bits of the interview that belong in dialogue. But another editing technique produces the dramatic difference between the two versions: the first is a single, page-long paragraph; the second has been broken up into more manageable chunks. The second version has white space.

At the beginning of *Alice in Wonderland,* Alice glances at a book her sister is reading, notices it has no illustrations or dialogue, and thinks, "And what is the use of a book without pictures or conversations?" If you've ever leafed through a book in a bookstore and noticed page after page of long, dense paragraphs, you probably know how Alice felt. Before you've read a word, you're turned off.

So be on the lookout for paragraphs that run more than, say, a half-page in length. Whether it's because readers feel lectured to, or because they feel crowded, or simply because some white space on the page is visually inviting, lengthy unbroken chunks of written material are off-putting. The simple, purely mechanical change of paragraphing more frequently can make your writing much more engaging.

Paragraphing frequently can also add tension to a scene. In the example above, although the dialogue was all potentially there in the single paragraph, it didn't convey the tension between the two men until it was edited into a series of rapid-fire questions followed by two- and three-word answers. Whether it's because sentences tend to grow shorter as the speakers become more upset, or simply because read-

"The Publisher has asked Granville to be on the lookout for paragraphs that run more than a half page in length."

ers' eyes move down the page more quickly, frequent paragraphing gives dialogue snap and momentum.

Many writers who write thrillers seem to use this technique instinctively. Consider this passage from Elmore Leonard's *La Brava:*

La Brava said, "You know the big blond guy."

"The Silver Kid," Paco said, "of course."

"I want somebody to deliver a note to him, at his hotel."

"Sure."

"And write it."

"What does it say?"

"I want him to come to the park tonight, 1:00 A.M., across from the Play House Bar."

"Sign your name?"

"No, sign it C.R."

"Just C.R.?"

"That's the *Marielito,* the one with the earring."

"Oh," Paco said, "yes, I remember."

"But I have to make sure the big blond guy gets the message and not the police."

Paco said, "Man, you got something going on."

"If I can, I'd like to get a hold of a baseball bat," La Brava said. "But I think the stores are closed."

"You and this guy going to play ball? In the dark? Never mind, don't tell me," Paco said. "I got one for softball you can use."

"I'll take good care of it."

Not that you're going to want to maintain this sort of pace for very long. A novel that is literally a page-turner beginning to end is more likely to leave its readers feeling weary—and manipulated—than satisfied. When you want to create a more relaxed mood, or give your readers a chance to breathe (or reflect), or simply lull them into complacency before you spring something on them, try paragraphing a little less frequently than usual. John le Carré uses the technique to great effect in *The Secret Pilgrim:*

> Two armchairs stood before a dying fire. One was empty. I took it to be the Professor's. In the other, somewhat obscured from my line of sight, sat a silky, rounded man of forty with a cap of soft black hair and twinkling round eyes that said we were all friends, weren't we? His winged chair was high-backed and he had fitted himself into the angle of it like an aircraft passenger prepared for landing. His rather circular shoes stopped short of the floor, and it occurred to me they were East European shoes: marbled, of an uncertain leather, with molded, heavy-treaded soles. His hairy brown suit was like a remodeled military uniform. Before him stood a table with a pot of mauve hyacinths on it, and beside the hyacinths lay a display of objects which I recognized as the instruments of silent killing: two garrotes made of wooden toggles and lengths of piano wire; a screwdriver so sharpened that it was a stiletto; a Charter Arms .38 Undercover revolver with a five-shot cylinder, together with two kinds of bullet, six soft-nosed and six rifled, with congealed powder squashed into the grooves.
>
> "It is cyanide," the Professor explained, in answer to my silent perplexity.

The leisurely and soft-edged tone to the details help lull the reader into a relaxed moment—to a purpose, since we are being set up. But what greatly supports this aim is the writer's use of a long paragraph, in effect keeping us in that chair until he's ready to spring the cyanide on us.

You can also focus attention on some important development by placing it in its own short paragraph. Consider this chapter ending from Gloria Murphy's *Down Will Come Baby*. Amelia is thirteen, drunk, and drowning. Robin has just swum out to rescue her.

> "Stop it!" Robin screamed, but Amelia was too terrified to hear her. She pounced on Robin's back, her arms clasped tightly around her neck, and dragged her down. Robin fought to free herself, but it was as though strong tentacles were pulling her deeper and deeper.
>
> It wasn't until she swallowed the second mouthful of water that Robin stopped the struggle. Then slowly, slowly, wrapped together like sleeping Siamese twins, they began to drift upward. When they finally broke the surface, Robin took a gasp of air, turned, swung her arm out, and bashed Amelia in the face. Amelia let go.
>
> Robin—choking and gagging, barely able to tread water—watched as Amelia sank for the last time, her eyes pleading with Robin to let her die.

Now try this version:

> "Stop it!" Robin screamed, but Amelia was too terrified to hear her. She pounced on Robin's back, her arms clasped tightly around her neck, and dragged her

down. Robin fought to free herself, but it was as though strong tentacles were pulling her deeper and deeper.

It wasn't until she swallowed the second mouthful of water that Robin stopped the struggle. Then slowly, slowly, wrapped together like sleeping Siamese twins, they began to drift upward. When they finally broke the surface, Robin took a gasp of air, turned, swung her arm out, and bashed Amelia in the face.

Amelia let go.

The first version was well-written and exciting. But the second, by focusing all the horror of Amelia's death into that single, three-word paragraph, ends the chapter with a dramatic punch that the first version lacks. And the only difference between the two is the extra paragraph and the cut.

Dialogue also adds white space, or at least it should. So when you reread a scene or chapter, be on the lookout for places where your characters make little speeches to one another. In formal dialogue, characters often string together four or five complete, well-formed sentences. In real life, few of us get that far without interruption. So break your dialogue up, write in more give-and-take between your characters, have your characters interrupt one another—and themselves. Let them mix it up a little, or a lot.

Of course, sometimes it's *appropriate* for a character to make a speech, in which case a long paragraph may be effective. In the scene quoted in the last chapter from Frederick Buechner's *Treasure Hunt,* Brownie has told the narrator that he never really lived the life that Bebb gave him back and so has lost his faith. Following the little speech he makes

about that—a speech the writer wisely leaves in one piece—
the give-and-take of *dialogue* reasserts itself, all the more
effectively for Brownie's having been allowed to spill over:

He said, "Another thing, I have carnal desires like
everybody else, dear. Maybe you wouldn't believe it to
look at me, but I've had many opportunities for
backsliding in that direction here on the ranch. These
Indians, they don't mean any harm by it, but lots of
times they don't care a fig what they do or who they do
it with just as long as they get a chance to do it. It's like
when you've got a healthy young appetite, you'll take
anything that's put before you. I've always resisted these
temptations because of my faith. I've passed up things
that . . . joys . . ." He took off his glasses and rubbed
his eyes with his thumb and forefinger. He said, "Now I
ask myself this question. All these precious things I've
given up for Jesus, what have I got to show for it?"

I said, "Brownie, your interpretations of scripture
bring lots of people comfort and hope."

He said, "Scripture says, 'Cast thy bread upon the
waters for thou shalt find it after many days.' I have cast
my whole life upon the waters, and it's sunk out of
sight like a stone."

"Nobody knows you've lost your faith, Brownie.
You can keep on helping people anyway. That way you
might get it back again."

He said, "You don't know how it feels to say things
you don't believe any more. It's like a woman with a
dead baby inside her."

In *I Never Promised You a Rose Garden,* Hannah Green puts the theme of the novel into the mouth of a psychiatrist—suddenly confronted by her patient's awareness of injustice within the "safe" world of the mental hospital—and gives it its own paragraph:

"Helene kept her bargain about Ellis and so did I," Deborah said. "What good is your reality then?"

"Look here," Furii said. "I never promised you a rose garden. I never promised you perfect justice . . . [or] peace or happiness. My help is so that you can be free to fight for all of those things. The only reality I offer is challenge, and being well is being free to accept it or not at whatever level you are capable. I never promise lies, and the rose-garden world of perfection is a lie . . . and a bore, too!"

"Will you bring it up at the meeting—about Helene?"

"I said I would and I will, but I promise nothing."

And in this passage from *Dinner at the Homesick Restaurant,* you can see how the writer uses both short and long paragraphs for effect in the same scene. Anne Tyler surrounds two spillover speeches—by a father and son who haven't seen each other in twenty-five years—with a series of one-line paragraphs:

"You left us in her clutches," Cody said.

Beck looked up. He said, "Huh?"

"How could you do that?" Cody asked him. "How

could you just dump us on our mother's mercy?" He bent closer, close enough to smell the camphorish scent of Beck's suit. "We were kids, we were only kids, we had no way of protecting ourselves. We looked to you for help. We listened for your step at the door so we'd be safe, but you just turned your back on us. You didn't lift a finger to defend us."

Beck stared past Cody at the traffic.

"She wore me out," he told Cody finally.

"Wore you out?"

"Used up my good points. Used up all my good points."

Cody straightened.

"Oh, at the start," Beck said, "she thought I was wonderful. You ought to have seen her face when I walked into a room. When I met her, she was an old maid already. She'd given up. No one had courted her for years, her girlfriends were asking her to baby-sit, their children called her Aunt Pearl. Then I came along. I made her so happy! There's my downfall, son. I just can't resist a person I make happy. I expect if I'd got that divorce from your mother I'd have married six times over, just moving on to each new woman that cheered up some when she saw me, moving on again when she got close to me and didn't act so pleased any more. Oh, it's closeness that does you in. Never get too close to people, son—did I tell you that when you were little? When your mother and I were first married, everything was perfect. It seemed I could do no wrong. Then bit by bit I guess she saw my faults. I'd never hid them, but now it seemed they mattered after all. She saw that I was away from home too much, didn't get ahead in my work, put on weight, talked wrong, dressed wrong, drove a car wrong. I'd bring home a simple toy, say, and it would somehow start a fight—your mother saying it was too expensive or too dangerous, and the three of you kids bickering over who got to play with it first . . ."

Up until now, we've talked about breaking up your writing on the level of paragraphs. But the same principle applies on a larger scale—mechanical decisions about the length of your scenes or chapters can give you more control over your story. Brief scenes or even brief chapters can add to your story's tension, and longer chapters can give it a more leisurely feel. Scenes and chapters have a rhythm.

That rhythm should not be unvaried. Some writers tend to fall into a rut—like the one mentioned in chapter 1, whose scenes were all about five minutes long. And in some cases, the steady rhythm of similarly sized scenes or chapters can reinforce a story's steady forward momentum. But if the scene or chapter length remains steady while the tension of the story varies considerably, you are passing up the chance to reinforce the tension your story depends on. You are failing to use one of the simplest of storytelling tools.

Checklist

- Flip through your manuscript without even reading it—just notice the white space. How much of it is there? Do you have any paragraphs that go on as much as a page in length? A lot of paragraphs that run longer than a half-page?
- If one of your scenes seem to drag, try paragraphing a little more often.
- Do you have scenes with *no* longer paragraphs? Remember, what you're after is the right balance.
- Have your characters made little speeches to one another?
- If you're writing a novel, are all your scenes or chapters exactly the same length?

Exercises

A.   *More playing with real writers. Take this passage from Garrison Keillor's* Leaving Home *and adjust the paragraphing to give it more drive:*

It has been a quiet week in Lake Wobegon. Sunday morning Clarence Bunsen stepped into the shower and turned on the water—which was cold, but he's Norwegian, he knows you have to take what you can get—and stood until it got warm, and he was reaching for the soap when he thought for sure he was having a heart attack. He's read a *Reader's Digest* story about a man's heart attack ("My Most Unforgettable Experience") and this felt like the one in the story—chest pain like a steel band tightening. Clarence grabbed the nozzle as the rest of the story flashed before his eyes: the ride in the ambulance, the dash to the emergency room, unconsciousness as the heart team worked over him, the long slow recovery and the discovery of a new set of values. But as he imagined what was about to happen, the heart attack petered out on him. The story said it felt like an elephant stepping on you. This felt more like a big dog, and then somebody whistled and the dog left. So it wasn't a heart attack, there was no story, and Clarence felt better.

B.   *Read through this passage and note where you might paragraph it differently (be warned, the changes that will make a difference are subtle):*

Jeanine stared at the spider plant hung over the kitchen sink. Most of its leaves were yellow and a few were going brown at the edges. "I don't believe this," she said.

"What?" Ed said.

"I only gave you this plant a month ago, and look at it now." She reached out and tenderly touched one of the leaves. It came off in her hand. "I mean, this is a spider plant. You can't kill these things, they thrive on neglect. How did you manage to do this much damage so quickly?" She stuck one finger in the potting soil.

"I don't know. I've been watering it once a week, just like you said. I've even been using plant food I picked up at the hardware store the other day. It's that blue powder that dissolves in water, one tablespoon to the quart."

"Ed, let me see that plant food." He opened the cupboard under the sink, rummaged for a moment, and came up with a box with a picture on the front. She took it and scanned the instructions. "According to this, you're supposed to use one teaspoon to the quart."

"Oh, well, I guess that explains it then."

Chapter 10

ONCE IS
USUALLY ENOUGH

[D]espite its tireless narrative energy, despite its
relentless inventiveness, the book is bloated, grown to
elephantine proportions. . . . Repetition is the problem;
the same stories are told several times, accruing more
detail with each telling. Also, the principal characters
have a way of regurgitating what they've learned, even
though the reader was with them when they learned it.

—PATRICK MCGRATH, *in a* New York Times *review of*
The Witching Hour, *by Anne Rice*

The problem Mr. McGrath describes is one we see regularly in the writing of both novices and professionals: unintentional repetition. Most writers already know to edit out
places where they have literally repeated a word or phrase.
But the repetition of an *effect* can be just as problematic.
Whether it's two sentences that convey the same information, two paragraphs that establish the same personality

trait, or two characters who fill the same role in the plot, repetition can rob your writing of its power.

Even experienced writers have occasional trouble with repetition, usually because they're too close to what they've accomplished with their writing to spot the places where they've accomplished it twice. (Once again, putting your work in a drawer for a couple of weeks is a good way to see it afresh.) But more often repetition of effect shows up in the fiction of novices. The reason is a lack of confidence on the writer's part. After all, it takes quite a bit of experience and insight to judge exactly what impact your writing will have on your readers. So when you have a character point or plot development that is critical to the story, you drive it home more than once to make sure your readers get it.

But chances are good that you've underestimated your readers' intelligence or your own ability or both. As a result, you wind up conveying to your readers things they already know, which is almost as condescending (and off-putting) as describing emotions that have already been shown in the dialogue. Consider the following from a workshop submission:

> By this time, Jerry wished he could bring his
> Mustang to his father's garage near Tralee. He missed
> his father's garage. It was a small, cluttered shop off the
> main road, and sometimes he ached to be there. He
> remembered throwing down his books after school and
> running back to the garage to do a little "jobeen" for his
> father. Picking his way through the parts, handing his
> father particular wrenches, listening to his dad's Irish
> names for parts of the car: *roth* for wheel, *coisceain* for

brakes, *inneal* for engine. He remembered especially his father's Irish phrase for carburetor: *croi an innill,* the heart of the engine, the heart of the machine. He missed all this, and wondered why he'd ever left.

Here the writer is trying too hard to impress us with how much Jerry misses his father's garage—we're told about it no less than three times. The writer doesn't have to tell us even once. The description shows how much Jerry missed the place, as you can see from a version with the repetitions removed:

> By this time, Jerry wished he could bring his Mustang to his father's garage near Tralee, the small, cluttered shop off the main road where he used to throw down his books after school and run in to do a little "jobeen" for his father. Pick his way through the parts, hand his father particular wrenches, learn his dad's Irish names for parts of the car: *roth* for wheel, *coisceain* for brakes, *inneal* for engine. He remembered especially his father's phrase for carburetor: *croi an innill,* the heart of the engine, the heart of the machine.

Besides the condescension involved, repeating an effect simply doesn't work. In fact, repetition is likely to weaken rather than intensify the power of that effect. Take a look at this excerpt from a dinner scene by one of the authors:

> "It's enough just to be here. With you." She took his hands in hers and played with them while she

talked. "We can be by ourselves later, we can make love and sleep and make more love—later. Right now this is all I can hold."

It was enough for him, too. He feasted on the sight of her taking big bites of the veal, washing them down with long, long swallows of wine.

By the time the second course had been served, she was pronouncing her words very, very carefully. And when she excused herself to go to the ladies' room, she kept bumping into the tables to the right and left of her.

Notice that the writer tells us the heroine took long, long swallows of wine and then conveys her inebriation in two ways—the careful pronunciation and the staggering. But the staggering (which is a cliché) tends to detract from the careful pronunciation (which is fresher and more effective). When you try to accomplish the same effect twice, the weaker attempt is likely to undermine the power of the stronger one. Inspired by a very gifted novelist-client who is also a gifted writing instructor, we often write a formula in the margin of manuscripts: $1 + 1 = \frac{1}{2}$.

Or take another example, this one lifted from one of our favorite five-page workshop submissions. Rita is the narrator's oldest friend. She is also a ghost:

There are times I'm glad no one but me sees Rita, like when we hit the bars. In spite of her size, Rita still thinks of herself as a sexy broad. She wears long dangling gold earrings, rhinestone baubles that twinkle too much to pass for the real thing. And she shows too much bust. Now when you weigh almost two hundred pounds, any bust is too much in my opinion, but Rita doesn't see it that way. I guess it goes with her tiger-striped dresses and red hair. Now I know what you are thinking, why should a spook have dyed hair? But who am I to deny the black roots in Rita's coiffure?

The writer conveys Rita's habit of gaudy dress three times, and although each instance reads delightfully, the cumulative effect is still to weaken the whole—as can be seen from a look at the passage with the one-plus-ones edited out:

> There are times I'm glad no one but me sees Rita, like when we hit the bars. She wears long dangling gold earrings, and she shows too much bust. Now, when you weigh two hundred pounds, any bust showing is too much in my opinion, but Rita doesn't see it that way. I guess it goes with her tiger-striped dress and dyed hair.
>
> I don't expend any energy wondering why a ghost should have dyed hair—who am I to deny Rita's roots?

One form of repetition that we've seen more often in recent years is the use of brand names to help characterization. The mention of what type of scotch your hero drinks or what kind of car your heroine drives may help give your readers a handle on their personalities. But when all your characters glance at their Rolexes, then hop into their Maseratis to tear out to the house in the Hamptons, where they change out of their Armanis and pour themselves a

Glenlivet—you've gone too far. You don't want to sound as though you used a Sharper Image catalogue for a thesaurus.

We once worked on a manuscript in which the hero drove a Porsche Targa. Evidently this was the writer's dream car, because he mentioned it every chance he got. After forty or fifty pages of "hopping into the Targa," and "taking the Targa to the Hendricks'," and "running the Targa out to Long Island," we took to writing "Just call it the car!" in the margins.

Interior monologue is also prone to needless repetition, possibly because our thoughts tend to run in circles when we're upset. True, sometimes you can capture a character's mood by showing his or her thoughts chasing their tails, but more often than not, repetition in interior monologue is like rambling, repetitive dialogue—authentic but tedious. Consider this passage taken from an unpublished novel in which the heroine's lover and (her) children have left the campsite—and the heroine:

> What was the matter with her? What was stopping her from stopping *them*? All she had to do was say she was sorry—for something, for anything—to make it all right, have him come back and hold her, hold them all in his large embrace. *I'm sorry for* . . . what? She looked at the packet of dried milk that lay on the ground and couldn't think of one single thing to be sorry for. She stirred the damn ground turkey, which would remain tasteless no matter how much garlic she put in and which now nobody would eat and which she would not throw away no matter how much she hated it. She

could never bring herself to waste anything. She was a saver, a keeper, had kept herself and the children all those first years, alone.

Now read the passage with the one-plus-ones pared down to ones, and you can see that the interior monologue takes on a new strength. Notice especially the power of the last line, which in the unedited version was all but effaced by the sentence that preceded it:

> What was stopping her from stopping *them*? All she had to do was say she was sorry to make it all right, make him come back and hold her, hold them all in his large embrace. *I'm sorry for* . . . what?
> She looked at the packet of dried milk that lay broken at her feet and couldn't think of one single thing to be sorry for. She stirred the damned ground turkey, which would remain tasteless no matter how much garlic she put in it and which she would not throw away no matter how much she hated it. She was a saver, a keeper, had kept herself and the children all those first years, alone.

Incidentally, note that the phrase "on the ground" has been changed to "at her feet" because the "ground" of the campsite and the "ground turkey" are only a sentence apart. Keep an eye out for unconscious repetitions on the smallest scale—especially repetitions in which the repeated word isn't used in the same sense as the original word. ("She heard a sharp crack, the loud spring of her bedsprings.")

But also note that in the edited campsite passage above, "stopping," "make," "hold," and "sorry" are all repeated, and to good effect. There is also deliberate (and effective) repetition in the three phrases strung together about the fate of the ground turkey. A fringe benefit of getting rid of unnecessary repetitions is that it frees up the power of intentional repetitions, or repetitions for effect.

Why would you want to repeat an effect? If a given plot point or character attribute is sufficiently subtle or powerful, it may pay to approach it from two different directions. Or you may use different approaches to the same point to introduce new insights, a literary version of the cinematic *Rashomon* technique. And your repetition for effect will be that much stronger if there are no needless repetitions, as in this passage from Laurie Colwin's *Happy All the Time,* in which the writer builds a cumulative picture of a character through repetition of effect:

> She never smiled, that Vincent could see. In fact,
> she appeared to spend her life in a sort of tear. In the
> morning, she stormed into her office wearing a green
> suede coat that she threw onto a chair. When she was
> working, she muttered to herself, broke pencils, and
> threw them on the floor. She often swore horribly.
> When she condescended to bid Vincent good morning,
> she did so in a hostile whisper.

There's another fringe benefit to learning to watch for repetition. As you come to see what each element of your story—each sentence, each paragraph—accomplishes, you can learn to accomplish more than one thing at a time. While there is nothing wrong with having some sentences or paragraphs or scenes that do only one thing—a beat that captures your character's mood, dialogue that establishes a given character trait, a scene that sets up an upcoming plot twist—real life is more complex than that. And you can make your fictional world seem more like the real world by working in some interrelatedness.

We've already mentioned using descriptions not only to introduce readers to your settings but to convey your characters. Similarly, you can write an encounter that doesn't just advance the plot but also shows a tender side of one of your minor characters as well. Or you can use a scene to show us some vital clue about the killer and involve your detective more deeply in a moral dilemma. If each element of your story accomplishes one thing and one thing only, then your story will subtly, almost subliminally, feel artificial. When everything seems to be happening at once, then it will feel like real life.

To show that reviewers notice repetition problems, consider this from a review by Carolyn See of Tim Paulson's *The Real World:*

> This is a paean to dullness and inattention to detail . . . So what if on Page 117 Tom's sister "hams up" her Southern accent and on Page 119 Mac Stuart "hams up" a Southern accent? So what if on Page 134, after Tom and Julie move to Brooklyn, "their *real friends* braved the three subway transfers" and on Page 335 Tom remarks: "We found out who our *real friends*

are when they come to see us"? This is the real world, for Pete's sake! And whoever said the real world was anything more than dull, repetitive, and boring?

Up until now, we've been talking about small-scale repetition—repeating an effect two or more times within a scene or chapter. But as you revise, be on the lookout for unwarranted repetition on the larger scale as well. When you write two or more chapters that accomplish the same thing, or when you have two or more characters who play the same role in the story, you dissipate your writing just as much as when you have two sentences or paragraphs that accomplish the same thing. On all scales, it's better to do it once and do it well than to do it twice.

We once worked with a writer whose hero was being stalked by a person or persons unknown for reasons equally unknown. In the process of discovering who was trying to kill him and why, the hero received help from a buddy from Vietnam, an old school friend, the friend's wife (who had Mafia connections), and a Mafia don. The plot was already well supplied with characters, and now here were four more, all of them being put to essentially the same purpose.

We suggested character-combining, and the writer liked the idea. When he was done, the old school friend and his wife were gone, the Vietnam buddy and the Mafia don had taken over the wife's and friend's part in the plot, and the story was easier to follow and more fun to read. The writer had, in effect, been using four characters to do the work of two.

"Wendeke's hero is being stalked by a person or persons unknown for reasons equally unknown..."

While you're looking at the big picture, also bear in mind that there are some effects that will work no more than once in an entire novel. Having your hero become sick to his stomach can be a good way to show he is upset, for instance. But *Spy* magazine once collected all of the passages from Julia Phillips's *You'll Never Eat Lunch in This Town Again* in which her characters threw up for various reasons. After reading all these passages in a row (there were about twenty of them), you were glad you never had to eat in Hollywood—and, probably, resolved not to read *You'll Never Eat Lunch in This Town Again.*

Another way in which writers indulge in large-scale overkill is in the creation of characters. When you're trying to create a distinctive or eccentric character, it's not hard to slip over the line into stereotype or cartoon. We once worked with a writer on a suspense novel that involved a serial killer in a college town in the Midwest. The killer and the police chief tracking him were well-drawn characters of considerable depth; the murders, truly harrowing. But the writer decided he needed some comic relief, for which purpose he added a foolish college president, a vain trustee, a militant student, and a dim-witted custodian. Since all four of these characters were more cartoons than flesh and blood, they stuck out against the backdrop of realistically drawn characters. Their purpose in the story was obvious, and the good idea (the novel *did* need some comic relief) was undone by overkill.

Again, when you overdo some aspect of your novel for effect, the effect you are likely to get may be just the opposite of the one you intended. This is particularly true in the creation of heavies. Far too often, fictional antagonists are so thoroughly evil, so rapacious or sadistic or egomaniacal, that they cease to be frightening. The most frightening heavies, of course, are those readers can understand and identify with on some level. Cartoons, even evil cartoons, aren't nearly as frightening as real human beings.

Gloria Murphy uses this principle to striking effect in *Nightshade,* in which the villain kidnaps a woman's two children and holds them hostage to attract her to a cabin in the

Maine woods. Once there, she discovers his true purpose: to have the family he never had. The man is a psychopath, and his pathology is truly frightening—years earlier, he murdered the woman's first husband and raped her—but he's also a character we can identify with on some level. After all, the only thing he wants is a family of his own.

Then there is repetition on the largest scale, from book to book. We once worked with a writer on an unusual, well-written novel about a rich, upper-class gentleman in San Francisco who falls in love with a dirt-poor, endearing Chinese woman. Their love affair, having destroyed his marriage and career, eventually breaks apart thanks to incompatibilities between the lovers' Eastern and Western sensibilities.

As developed, the theme and plot are wonderfully engaging. But in the writer's second novel, a passionate love affair between a rich Westerner and a charming Japanese woman eventually breaks up thanks to East-West incompatibility. And at the heart of the third book lies a romance between a rich Westerner and a Korean woman . . . you get the picture.

Of course, there is room in the world of fiction for the formulaic novel—it's been said that every James Bond novel has the same plot. But when you repeat the same character under different names in several of your novels, or invoke the same clever plot twist more than once, you are weakening the effectiveness of what you've created just at the point where you most want to be original.

Many of the self-editing points in this book reflect changes in stylistic fashion—beginning, if you recall, with showing and telling. But the "once is (usually) enough" principle has apparently been valid for more than a century. Consider this from Mark Twain's review of James Fenimore Cooper's Leatherstocking novels:

> In his little box of stage properties [Cooper] kept six or eight cunning devices, tricks, artifices for his savages and woodsmen to deceive and circumvent each other with, and he was never so happy as when he was working these innocent things and seeing them go. A favorite one was to make a moccasined person tread in the tracks of the moccasined enemy, and thus hide his own trail. Cooper wore out barrels and barrels of moccasins in working that trick. Another stage-property that he pulled out of his box pretty frequently was his broken twig. . . . It is a restful chapter in any book of his when somebody doesn't step on a dry twig. . . . In fact, the Leather Stocking Series ought to have been called the Broken Twig Series.

Checklist

- Reread your manuscript, keeping in mind what you are trying to do with each paragraph—what character point you're trying to establish, what sort of mood you're trying to create, what background you're trying to suggest. In how many different ways are you accomplishing each of these ends?

- If more than one way, try reading the passage without the weakest approach and see if it isn't more effective.
- How about on the chapter level? Do you have more than one chapter that accomplishes the same thing?
- Is there a plot device or stylistic effect you are particularly pleased with? How often do you use it?
- Are your villains villainous in more than one way? Have you given them any characteristics that will allow your readers to identify with them?
- Finally, keep on the lookout for unintentional word repeats. Remember, the more striking a word or phrase is, the more jarring it will be if you repeat it.

Exercises

A.   *Trim the repetition out of the following:*

"Come on in, don't be bashful."

It wasn't exactly bashfulness that was keeping me in the hallway. This was my first visit to a bachelor's apartment, and I was shocked at how much it lived up to the reputation. It wasn't just the velvet painting of Elvis on the wall above the blue velvet couch, or the orange shag rug, or the

Formica coffee table, or the wall unit that looked like it was made of genuine simulated plastic wood. It was the sense that the place had been lived in, and lived in hard.

There were nicks in the top of the coffee table that looked as if they might have been caused by tap shoes. There was also a small collection of cigarette burns on one arm of the dark brown vinyl recliner in front of the TV. The TV antenna was a bent coat hanger with an undershirt hanging from it. Presumably a dirty undershirt—I didn't want to get close enough to check. Also, there were one or two unidentified stains on the ceiling.

"Like it?" he said. "I spent all day yesterday cleaning it up, just for you."

B. *Then there's this description, from an early draft of* A Reasonable Madness *by Fran Dorf:*

Clancy is a referral from Marilyn Reinhold via Donald Grayson via Rose Sumner. Frankly, I'm ashamed of my colleagues, passing the man around that way, not that I don't understand it. It's just that Clancy's so damned *boring*. I guess my colleagues feel there are so many interesting people in this city who get into therapy—homosexual television producers, actresses sleeping their way to the top, hot shot agency heads, philandering Wall Street dynamos—that it's not necessary to suffer through a patient like Clancy. It *is* tempting to

turn him away, I've thought about it myself.
Clancy's an accountant for a small rock salt
distributor in Queens. He's a pale and timid man
with a vapid smile and a nasal, rambling speaking
style, so slow you could fall asleep before he gets
the next word out. Particularly annoying is his
undying allegiance to his employer of ten years
who pays him at the end of that loyal service the
great sum of $42,000 per year, and who expects
overtime without pay on a consistent basis.
Clancy's really a very nice man, but his problems
are small, *small,* and boring.

Chapter 11

SOPHISTICATION

As she walked toward the kitchen, Heather peeled off various items of clothing. The image she projected of neatness, she thought, was just that—an image. Heather was a slob at heart.

Stopping in the entranceway to the kitchen, she leaned against the door frame and peeled off her panty hose. As she tossed them toward the top of the refrigerator, she breathed a sigh of relief. She was still hot, but at least she was free of the confines of clothing. Now for something to eat, she thought as she stood in front of the refrigerator.

You're likely to have spotted a couple of self-editing problems (such as the repetition and unneeded thinker attributions) in the above passage. And correcting for the self-editing points we have covered so far will help make any writing seem more professional. But you can also easily learn a few stylistic tricks that will lend your writing that extra bit of sophistication that gives it an edge. These tricks range from avoiding legitimate constructions that have been over-used by hack writers to finding alternatives to certain stylis-tic techniques that have virtually disappeared over the last few decades. Whatever it is that makes your mechanics sophisticated, awareness of them when revising will help your work look like that of a professional rather than an amateur.

One easy way to make your writing seem more sophisti-cated is to avoid two stylistic constructions that are common to hack writers, namely:

> **Pulling off her gloves,** she turned to face him.

and:

> **As she pulled off her gloves,** she turned to face him.

Both the *as* construction and the *-ing* construction as used above are grammatically correct and express the action clearly and unambiguously. But notice that both of these constructions take a bit of action ("She pulled off her gloves") and tuck it away into a dependent clause ("Pulling off her gloves . . ."). This tends to place some of your action at one remove from your reader, to make the actions seem incidental, unimportant. If you use these constructions often, you weaken your writing.

Another reason to avoid the *as* and *-ing* constructions is that they can give rise to physical impossibilities. We once worked on the autobiography of a behavioral biologist who, in the process of describing her field work, wrote, "Disappearing into my tent, I changed into fresh jeans." The *-ing* construction forced simultaneity on two actions that can't be simultaneous. The doctor didn't duck into the tent and pull on clean pants at the same time—she was a biologist, not a contortionist.

We're not suggesting that you avoid these phrases altogether. There are going to be times when you want to write about two actions that are actually simultaneous and/or genuinely incidental—actions that deserve no more than a dependent clause. And given the choice between an *as* or *-ing* construction and a belabored, artificial alternative, you're well advised to use the *as* or *-ing*. But be aware that hacks have long ago run these useful constructions into the ground. Learn to spot them in your own writing and, if you see more than one or two on a page, start hunting around for alternatives.

For instance, "Pulling off her gloves, she turned to face him" could easily be changed to "She pulled off her gloves and turned to face him," or even "She pulled off her gloves, turned to face him." Or you can make an *-ing* phrase less conspicuous by moving it to the middle of the sentence rather than the beginning, where it seems particularly amateurish.

To see just how much these constructions can weaken your writing, take a look at the rest of the scene we quoted at the beginning of the chapter, with the *as* and *-ing* constructions in boldface type:

Ripping off several large, dripping hunks of burrito, she pulled up a chair to the kitchen table and took a large bite. **As she chewed,** she wondered who she was maddest at. Clark, she decided.

The doorbell rang. "Heather, it's me!" boomed a deep, authoritative voice. "Clark!"

Spotting her favorite red silk kimono crumpled on the floor, Heather stooped over and picked it up. **As she pulled the kimono over her shoulders,** she said a prayer of thanks that the wrinkled look was in.

As her fingers unfastened the chain lock, she wondered how Clark had gotten her address. It wasn't listed in the telephone book.

"Good evening," Clark greeted with a small bow **as the door swung open.**

"The bug man came last week," Heather said sarcastically, **refusing to budge from the door.** "I thought he'd exterminated all the pests in my life, but I guessed he missed one. A big one."

"Funny, very funny," Clark said, clearly not amused **as he leaned an arm against the door jamb.** "Now you'd better let me in before I start causing a scene."

Now take a look at the same scene again, with the *as* and *-ing* clauses removed, along with some of the other self-editing problems (after all, "Clark greeted" . . . ?):

She pulled up a chair to the kitchen table and took a large bite of the burrito she'd found behind the milk and orange juice bottles. Who was she maddest at? Probably Clark.

The doorbell rang. "Heather, it's me!"

Clark. It had to be.

Heather sighed, stooped over and picked up her red silk kimono from the floor. Thank God the wrinkled look was in. But how had Clark gotten her address? It wasn't listed in the telephone book.

"Good evening." He made a small bow.

Heather didn't budge from the door. "The bug man came last week. I thought he'd exterminated all the pests in my life, but I guess he must have missed a big one."

"Funny, very funny." Clark leaned an arm against the door jamb. "You'd better let me in before I start causing a scene."

Admittedly this still isn't deathless prose, but the editing *has* made the passage read a lot more professionally.

Another way to keep from looking like an amateur is to avoid the use of clichés. Virtually all clichés, of course, begin their life as original, effective expressions—so effective, in fact, that they got used until all the life went out of them. So if you come across lifeless passages, you may need to self-edit for the purpose of weeding out any clichés. Your characters should never *live life in the fast lane,* nor should anything in your writing be *worth no more than a plugged nickel.* And if you come across "She tossed her head," the first question you should ask is, "How far?"

Watch for clichés on the larger scale, too, particularly in

the creation of minor characters. Don't outfit your account-ants in Coke-bottle glasses and pocket protectors, or make your clergymen mild and soft-spoken, or let your New York cabbies drive like maniacs (although, arguably, this last example is nothing more than simple verisimilitude). When you fall into characterization clichés like these, the result is a cartoon rather than a character.

There is one caveat: in narration, there may be times when you need to use a familiar, pet phrase—yes, a cliché—to summarize a complicated situation. But before going with the cliché, give some thought to the possibility of "turning" it, altering it slightly to render the phrasing less familiar. In a celebrated novel we edited, the writer used the phrase "they vanished into thin air" to avoid a lengthy, complicated explanation. We suggested a change to "they vanished into thick air," which fit the poetic, steamy atmo-sphere of the European city in which the scene was set.

In chapter 5, we warned you to watch out for *-ly* adverbs when you're writing dialogue. But even when you're not writing dialogue, be on the lookout for *-ly* adverbs, for the sake of sophistication. Chances are, as you bang out your first draft, you use the first verbs that come to mind—verbs that are commonplace and comfortable, verbs you don't have to dig too deep to find. *Set,* for instance, as in:

"She set the cup and saucer on the kitchen table."

Then, since *set* doesn't really convey what you want, you find the extra nuance you need in an adjective, tack on an *-ly* to make an adverb, and hook it to the verb.

"Angrily she set the cup and saucer on the kitchen table."

This approach may be all right for a first draft, but when you self-edit, you can root out these verb-adverb combinations like the weeds they are. The weak verbs that came to mind so readily can then be jettisoned in favor of stronger, more specific verbs—verbs that say exactly what you want to say without help.

"She slammed the cup and saucer onto the kitchen table."

When you use two words, a weak verb and an adverb, to do the work of one strong verb, you dilute your writing and rob it of its potential power.

There are exceptions, of course, as there are to every principle in this book. If your heroine has just finished the restoration of her 1952 MG-TD, a project she has been working on for the last nine years, you might be compelled to write:

"She tightened the last nut—slowly, lovingly."

It's not terrific writing but it's an understandable solution—there probably isn't a single verb in the English language than can convey this particular way of tightening a nut. But even where the adverbs aren't the product of lazy writing, they can still *look* like lazy writing, just because -*ly* adverbs have been used so often by so many hacks in the past. It might be better to rewrite the description of the car from your heroine's point of view and in her voice, so that we can see that she loves it, without your having to say so. To show rather than tell us.

A simple departure from conventional comma usage can also lend a modern, sophisticated touch to your fiction—especially your dialogue. All you have to do is string together short sentences with commas instead of separating them with periods, as in these examples:

> "I tried to tell him, I couldn't get his attention."
> "Hurry up, let's get going."
> "Don't worry about it, she's only sixteen."

This comma usage, if not overdone, conveys remarkably well the way speech actually falls on the ear. Most of us don't come to a full stop after every sentence when we're talking, nor do your characters have to. And this special effect needn't be reserved exclusively for dialogue passages. In *Billy Bathgate*, E. L. Doctorow often comma-strings sentences of narration:

> [He said] "Hey, young fellow, what's the younger generation reading these days?" as if it was really important to him. He turned the book up in my hand so he could read the title, I don't know what he expected, a French novel maybe, but he was genuinely surprised.

There are a few stylistic devices that are so "tacky" they should be used *very* sparingly, if at all. First on the list is emphasis quotes, as in the quotes around the word "tacky" in the preceding sentence. The only time you need to use them is to show you are referring to the word itself, as in the quotes around the word "tacky" in the preceding sentence. Read it again; it all makes sense.

Then there are the stylistic devices that make a writer look insecure, the most notable offenders being exclamation points and italics. Exclamation points are visually distracting and, if overused, are an irritation to readers. They should be reserved for moments when a character is physically shouting or experiencing the mental equivalent. When you use them *frequently,* you look as if you're trying *desperately* to infuse your dialogue or narration with an excitement it *lacks.* And, as you can see, frequent italics are the typographical equivalent of an elbow in the ribs and a frantic, "Did you *get* it? *Did* you?"

Articles and short stories in some romance magazines make such frequent use of italics and exclamation points that the result is a gushy, hyped-up style easy to parody:

> "Oh, *God!*" Samantha said, "do you know what he *did*? He picked me up and *threw* me onto the bed, and then he just *flung* himself on *top of me!* I tell you, Shirley, I was in seventh *heaven!*"

Should you need any further convincing on this point, note what happens to a poignant confrontation between mother and daughter in Mary Gordon's *The Company of Women* when we pump it up with just a few exclamation points and italics:

"I should never have let you go up there to Columbia. I should have known they'd take advantage of you!"

"*Nobody* took advantage of me, Mother."

"Then how did you get in this condition?" she said through her teeth.

"I got in this condition because I used the wrong kind of birth control!"

"Don't talk about that in this house!"

I had forgotten: in my mother's canon, practicing birth control was worse than having sex.

"Whose is it?" she asked. "That goddamned professor, right?"

"I'm not sure."

"Don't try and protect him. I *know* you."

"I'm not sure whose it is, Mother. I slept with two people. I'm not sure which one is the father!"

"Fine," said my mother. "Very nice. Just *beautiful!*"

That was the last she has ever spoken about the father of my child. There was not one *word* of forced marriages, not a mention of paternity suits. Which is remarkable, since she is, if nothing else, a woman who believes in convention.

Now read the passage as the writer wrote it:

"I should never have let you go up there to Columbia. I should have known they'd take advantage of you."

"Nobody took advantage of me, Mother."

"Then how did you get in this condition?" she said through her teeth.

"I got into this condition because I used the wrong kind of birth control."

"Don't talk about that in this house."

I had forgotten: in my mother's canon, practicing birth control was worse than having sex.

"Whose is it?" she asked. "That goddamned professor, right?"

"I'm not sure."

"Don't try and protect him. I know you."

"I'm not sure whose it is, Mother. I slept with two people. I'm not sure which one is the father."

"Fine," said my mother. "Very nice. Just beautiful."

That was the last she has ever spoken about the father of my child. There was not one word of forced marriages, not a mention of paternity suits. Which is remarkable, since she is, if nothing else, a woman who believes in convention.

You can see that the dialogue and description convey all the emotion needed. And the writer's voice, without the lexical trappings, is calm and confident.

There's another stylistic device whose overuse will brand you as an amateur: flowery, poetic figures of speech, much beloved by beginning writers and used very sparingly by the pros. If you're a poet, and most of your imagery is fresh and strong, reining yourself in may be more difficult than you might think. But unless your character is a poet and actually sees the world in poetic terms on an everyday basis, you need to do it. Otherwise, you're taking over your story from your characters, which is never a good idea.

Take a look at this excerpt from an early draft of Peter Cooper's novel *Billy Shakes,* in which a character has just learned that his wife is pregnant:

> "The trouble with women," Hoot said with a serious smile, "is that they always seem to think they have everything figured out. When the truth is, they don't know a thing."
>
> "Come on, Hoot," Lucy said. "Admit it. You're a father."
>
> "As a matter of fact, Lucy, it may be that Rose is pregnant." His eyes were a dark, dark blue, stolen jewels in a setting of bone. "But I can assure you that I am not the father."
>
> "What are you saying?" she asked in a horrified whisper.
>
> "I *can't* have children. That's what I'm saying." He paused to light a cigarette, his hand shaking ever so slightly. "It just so happens that I had a vasectomy a year before I married Rose."

The metaphor, the dark blue stolen jewels in a setting of bone, strains for effect. Yet the problem isn't the unworkability of the metaphor but its presence in the scene in the first place. This scene is the moment on which the plot of the entire novel turns—we find out in the next few paragraphs that Hoot's best friend, Lucy's husband, is the father of

Rose's child. Yet just when it's most important that we focus on events, we're pulled aside to notice the writer's poetic turn of mind. And like exclamation points or italics, phrases that call attention to themselves rather than to what's being said make it obvious that you're working hard for your effects.

When it comes to handling sex scenes, the last thing you want is to seem to be working hard to achieve your effects. The subtler stylistic approach will nearly always be the more professional looking choice. This means you'll want to avoid heavy breathing, whether it's the type appropriate to novels with titles like *Love's Helpless Fury* or the type common to novels with titles like *Motel Lust* or *Lust Motel.* There was a time when explicit sex scenes added a sense of sophistication, of authenticity to a book—to say nothing of boosting sales. But in a day when photographs that once would have been sold under the counter are used to advertise blue jeans, this approach has lost its power to shock or titillate.

The subtle approach, on the other hand, engages your reader's imagination and so is likely to be far more effective. This is an area where it might be a good idea to bring back an old-fashioned narrative convention: sexual encounters that take place in linespaces. After all, if you leave the physical details to your readers' imaginations, they are likely to be far more engaged than if you spell it all out. A linespace may be a far more erotic place for two characters to make love than a bed.

For instance, take a look at what is arguably the most

famous sex scene in modern literature, from Margaret Mitchell's *Gone With the Wind*:

He swung her off her feet and into his arms and started up the stairs. Her head was crushed against his chest and she heard the hard hammering of his heart beneath her ears. He hurt her and she cried out, muffled, frightened. Up the stairs he went in the utter darkness, up, up, and she was wild with fear. He was a mad stranger and this was a black darkness she did not know, darker than death. He was like death, carrying her away in arms that hurt. She screamed, stifled against him and he stopped on the landing and, turning her swiftly in his arms, bent over her and kissed her with a savagery and completeness that wiped out everything from her mind but the dark into which she was sinking and the lips on hers. He was shaking, as though he stood in a strong wind, and his lips, fallen from her body, fell on her soft flesh. He was muttering things she did not hear, his lips were evoking feelings never felt before. She was darkness and he was darkness and there had never been anything before this time, only darkness and his lips on hers. She tried to speak and his mouth was over her again. Suddenly she had a wild thrill such as she had never known; joy, fear, madness, excitement, surrender to arms that were too strong, lips too bruising, fate that moved too fast. For the first time in her life she had met someone, something stronger than she, someone she could neither bully nor break, someone who was bullying and breaking her. Somehow, her arms were around his neck and her lips trembling beneath his and they were going up, up into the darkness again, a darkness that was soft and swirling and all enveloping.

When she awoke the next morning, he was gone and had it not been for the rumpled pillow beside her, she would have thought the happenings of the night before a preposterous dream. . . .

A modern editor might break this up into another paragraph or two—we certainly would. But no editor in his or her right mind would add explicit sexual or anatomical details. The effectiveness of the scene in evoking the reader's imagination is as much in force today as it was in the late 1930s.

What is true of sexual details is also true of profanity. There was a time when your characters were convincingly worldly and streetwise if they swore a lot. But profanity has been so overused in past years that nowadays it's more a sign of a small vocabulary. Of course, if profanity is appropriate to your character, then have that character swear. But keep in mind that a moderate amount of profanity or obscenity can suggest a lot—your readers will get the idea. If you include a great deal of it, you're likely to turn them off. Just think about how much power a single obscenity can have if it's the only one in the whole fucking book.

"Since raw profanity and explicit sex scenes are no longer in vogue Maynard feels all his years of education and preparation were for naught."

The surest sign that you are achieving literary sophistication is when your writing begins to seem effortless. Not that it will *be* effortless, of course—crafting good prose is hard work. We often guide writers through four drafts before we see the novel published, even though the first draft we see may not be the first one the writer wrote.

And the goal of all this careful, conscious work is to produce a novel or short story collection that reads as though no hard labor were involved in producing it. Fred Astaire worked tirelessly to make dancing look like the easiest, most natural thing in the world. And that's what you're trying for—a level of effectiveness that can make what was hardest to achieve look effortless.

Checklist

- How many *-ing* and *as* phrases do you write? It may be time to get out the highlighter and mark them all. Remember, the only ones that count are the ones that place a bit of action in a subordinate clause.
- How about *-ly* adverbs? Both tied to your dialogue and within your descriptions and narration.
- Do you have a lot of short sentences, both within your dialogue and within your description and narration? Try stringing some of them together with commas.
- Do you use a *lot* of italics? And you don't use many exclamation points, do you?!
- Are there any figures of speech you're particularly proud of? Do they come at key moments during your plot? If so, think about getting rid of them.
- How much of your sex scenes do you leave to your readers' imaginations?
- Are you using a lot of profanity or obscenity?

Exercises

A.   *Edit this paragraph, taken from Kathleen E. Woodiwiss's* The Wolf and the Dove, *for sophistication (romance writers take note: Woodiwiss is a best-selling writer despite—not because of—her style):*

Grabbing up a pelt she pulled it close about her and gave him an impishly wicked look as she grinned. Turning on her heels with a low laugh, she went to the hearth, there to lay small logs upon the still warm coals. She blew upon them but drew back in haste as the ashes flew up and sat back upon her heels rubbing her reddened eyes while Wulfgar's amused chuckles filled the room. She made a face at his mirth and swung the kettle of water on its hook over the building heat as he crossed to the warmth of the fire beside her and began to dress.

B.   *A little historical editing. The stylistic conventions Lewis Carroll used in* Alice in Wonderland *were perfectly acceptable when he wrote it and don't really interfere with the genius of the book. But still they are clunky and cumbersome by today's standards. So try your hand at the following passage:*

All this time Tweedledee was trying his best to fold up the umbrella, with himself in it, which was such an extraordinary thing to do that it quite took off Alice's attention from the angry brother. But he couldn't quite succeed, and it ended in his rolling over, bundled up in the umbrella, with only his head out; and there he lay, opening and shutting his mouth and his large eyes—"looking more like a fish than anything else," Alice thought.

"Of course you agree to have a battle?" Tweedledum said in a calmer tone.

"I suppose so," the other sulkily replied, as he crawled out of the umbrella; "only *she* must help us dress up, you know."

So the two brothers went off hand in hand into the wood, and returned, in a minute, with their arms full of things—such as bolsters, blankets, hearthrugs, tablecloths, dish covers, and coal scuttles. "I hope you're a good hand at pinning and tying strings?" Tweedledum remarked. "Every one of these things has got to go on, somehow or other."

Alice said afterward she had never seen such a fuss made about anything in all her life—the way those two bustled about, and the quantity of things they put on, and the trouble they gave her in tying strings and fastening buttons—"Really, they'll be more like bundles of old clothes than anything else by the time they're ready!" she said to herself, as she arranged a bolster round the neck of

Tweedledee, "to keep his head from being cut off," as he said.

"You know," he added very gravely, "it's one of the most serious things that can possibly happen to one in a battle, to get one's head cut off."

C. *The Mother of All Exercises. This was written by one of the authors of this book as a workshop exercise. Be warned: every self-editing point we've mentioned in the book so far can be found in this one exercise.*

"But Ernestine, honey," Winthrop breathed, "I swear I was never anywhere near the John Smith motel!"

"Winthrop, *darling*," Ernestine said sarcastically, "that's not what I heard from Helena." She looked out the window.

Winthrop found himself looking at his hands. He scuffed the carpet with his foot, feeling like a small boy with a baseball bat in front of a broken window. But then his gorge began to rise at the injustice of it. "No!" he thought, defiant, "I intend to brazen it out." Helena Basquette was known to be the trouble-making type.

"Ernestine," he said sincerely. "You should have better sense than to trust to the ramblings of as big a fool as Helena Basquette. Why only last week . . ."

The doorbell rang resoundingly.

Laying her cigar carefully on the ashtray at her

arm, Ernestine crossed the room and opened the door.

The young man silhouetted against the streetlight was tall, his shock of black hair glimmering faintly with condensation from the evening fog. Over his lanky frame he wore a loose-fitting bomber jacket and faded, stone-washed jeans.

And in his hand, that familiar square box.

"You the guys that ordered the pizza?" he snarled.

Ernestine looked away. "Winthrop, sweetie," she continued bitingly, "are you responsible for this outrage?"

"Oh no," thought the pizza man. "He's been fightin' wid his old lady. I ain't gonna get no tip outta this one."

Chapter 12

VOICE

An early seafaring novel by a celebrated nineteenth-century novelist begins:

> It was the middle of a bright tropical afternoon that we made good our escape from the bay. The vessel we sought lay with her main-topsail aback about a league from the land and was the only object that broke the broad expanse of the ocean.

Years later the novelist wrote another first-person seafaring novel that begins:

> Call me Ishmael. Some years ago—never mind how long precisely—having little or no money in my purse, and nothing particular to interest me on shore, I thought I would sail about a little and see the watery part of the world.

The opening of *Omoo* raises some intriguing questions— Why does the narrator need to escape from the bay? Whom are the narrator and his companions escaping from?—and gives a clear and vivid picture of the waiting ship. The opening of *Moby-Dick* is irresistible. What makes the difference?

The answer, of course, is voice. And judging from these two Herman Melville novels, even the greatest voices develop over time. Certainly when he wrote *Omoo* Melville had not yet found what John Gardner (in *On Becoming a Novelist*) has called "his booming, authoritative voice." In the *Moby-Dick* opening, Gardner points out, the rhythms "lift and roll, pause, gather, roll again." The authority is unmistakable.

Of course, the writer's voice in a novel generally belongs to a character. The voice in *Moby-Dick* is Ishmael's as much as Melville's. But character voice and authorial voice are intimately connected, as you can see in the passages that follow in which we meet the protagonist in each novel:

> My name was Salmon, like the fish; first name,
> Susie. I was fourteen when I was murdered on
> December 6, 1973. In newspaper photos of missing
> girls from the seventies, most looked like me: white girls
> with mousy brown hair. This was before kids of all
> races and genders started appearing on milk cartons or
> in the daily mail. It was still back when people believed
> things like that didn't happen.
>
> In my junior high yearbook I had a quote from a
> Spanish poet my sister had turned me on to, Juan

Ramon Jimenez. It went like this: "If they give you ruled paper, write the other way." I chose it both because it expressed my contempt for structured surroundings in the classroom and because, not being some dopey quote from a rock group, I thought it marked me as literary. I was a member of the Chess Club and the Chem Club and burned everything I tried to make in Mrs. Delmonico's home ec class. My favorite teacher was Mr. Botte, who taught biology and liked to animate the frogs and crawfish we had to dissect by making them dance in their waxed pans. I wasn't killed by Mr. Botte, by the way.

—ALICE SEBOLD, *The Lovely Bones*

"Come, come," [Heathcliff] said, "you are flurried, Mr. Lockwood. Here, take a little wine. Guests are so exceedingly rare in this house that I and my dogs, I am willing to own, hardly know how to receive them. Your health, sir!"

I bowed and returned the pledge; beginning to perceive that it would be foolish to sit sulking for the misbehavior of a pack of curs: besides, I felt loath to yield the fellow further amusement at my expense; since the humor took that turn. He—probably swayed by prudential consideration of the folly of offending a good tenant—relaxed a little in the laconic style of clipping off his pronouns and auxiliary verbs, and introduced what he supposed would be a subject of interest to me—a discourse on the advantages and disadvantages of my place of retirement. I found him very intelligent on topics we touched; and before I went home, I was encouraged so far as to volunteer another visit tomorrow. He evidently wished no repetition of my intrusion. I shall go notwithstanding. It is astonishing how sociable I feel myself compared with him.

—EMILY BRONTË, *Wuthering Heights*

Somebody asked in English: "What did you say?"

Mr. Tench swiveled round. "You English?" he said in astonishment, but at the sight of the round and hollow face charred with a three days' beard, he altered his question: "You speak English?"

Yes, the man said, he spoke English. He stood stiffly in the shade, a small man dressed in a shabby dark city suit, carrying a small attaché case. He had a novel under his arm: bits of an amorous scene stuck out, crudely colored. He said: "Excuse me. I thought you were talking to me." He had protuberant eyes; he gave an impression of unstable hilarity, as if perhaps he had been celebrating a birthday . . . alone."

—GRAHAM GREENE, *The Power and the Glory*

Justin was standing with his elegant back to him. His neatly groomed head was turned to the wall. . . .

"Hi, Sandy," Justin said, drawing out the "Hi."

"Hi."

"I gather we're not assembling this morning. Trouble at mill?"

The famous golden voice, thought Woodrow, noticing every detail as if it were fresh to him.

Tarnished by time but guaranteed to enchant, as long as you prefer tone to substance. Why am I despising you when I'm about to change your life? From now until the end of your days there will be before this moment and after it and they will be separate ages for you, just as they are for me . . .

"And you're all well, I trust?" Justin asked in that same studied drawl of his. "Gloria not languishing in this awful heat? The boys both flourishing and so forth?"

"We're fine." A delay, of Woodrow's manufacture. "And Tessa is up-country," he suggested. He was giving her one last chance to prove it was all a dreadful mistake.

Justin at once became lavish, which was what he did when Tessa's name was spoken at him. "Yes, indeed. Her relief work is absolutely nonstop these days." He was hugging a United Nations tome to himself, all of three inches thick. Stooping again, he laid it to rest on a side table. "She'll have saved all Africa by the time we leave, at this rate."

"What's she gone up-country for actually?"—still clutching at straws—"I thought she was doing stuff down here in Nairobi. In the slums. Kibera, wasn't it?"

"Indeed she is," Justin said proudly. "Night and day, the poor girl. Everything from wiping babies' bottoms to acquainting paralegals with their civil rights, I'm told. Most of her clients are women, of course, which appeals to her. Even if it doesn't appeal quite so much to their menfolk." His wistful smile, the one that says *if only.* "Property rights, divorce, physical abuse, marital rape, female circumcision, safe sex. The whole menu, every day. You can see why their husbands get a little touchy, can't you? I would, if I was a marital rapist."

—JOHN LE CARRÉ, *The Constant Gardener*

A strong, distinctive, authoritative writing voice is something most fiction writers want—and something no editor or teacher can impart. There are, after all, no rules for writing like yourself. Voice is, however, something you can bring out in yourself. The trick is to not concentrate on it.

A famous poet giving a series of seminars was once asked to read a poem by one of his students. The poem was a long, self-conscious allegory in which various guests at a party represented different aspects of the student's life. The poet read it, then handed it back with the comment, "No, kid. First write rhymey-dimey stuff."

We recently worked with a novelist whose fiction featured a lot of short, punchy sentences and partial sentences ("It's a quarter after one. Almost time. He runs a fingernail over a rough gouge coursing across the face of his watch, implanted by something in his fall. It still runs."). The result was a distinctive, high-tension voice, one the writer had evidently worked hard to develop and maintain. Unfortunately, the voice was so distinctive that all of his characters sounded alike. And the tension stayed at such a high pitch for so long that the novel became exhausting to read. It was like hearing "The Flight of the Bumblebee" expanded to concert length.

It's perfectly understandable that a new writer could fall in love with the work of a brilliant literary figure (William Faulkner, say, or William Burroughs) and then try to emulate that literary voice. But when an amateur tries deliberately for the sort of mature voice found in seasoned professionals, the result is likely to be pretentious and largely unreadable. In fact, this sort of literary pretentiousness is another clear mark of an amateur.

And what usually gets imitated in literary homage is the writer's style, where the attempt (at least unconsciously) is to capture the writer's voice. Style and voice are not interchangeable. If you think about it, you can see that every writer has or can have a literary style, but by no means does every writer have a literary voice. Again, the way to develop voice is not by working on your style. Nor will using James Joyce's or Virginia Woolf's stylistic approaches give you their voices.

Bear in mind also that most of the great stylists have developed their style in the service of their stories. Faulkner does some daring and original things with point of view and even tense in *As I Lay Dying,* and the style serves the story of the Bundrens very well. But when he's telling a simpler, more straightforward story (as in *The Reivers*), he uses a more straightforward style. Remember, your primary purpose as a writer of fiction is to engage your readers in your story the best way you can. When your style starts to overshadow your story, it's defeating that purpose.

No, kid, first write rhymey-dimey stuff.

A warning, though. Don't let the danger of literary pretentiousness frighten you into a minimalism that doesn't fit your natural voice. There are times when poetic flights of fancy are appropriate, as with the James Joyce example from

"Remorse sits in my stomach like a piece of stale bread. How does that sound?"

chapter 6. Or consider this passage, from Edith Pargeter's *The Eighth Champion of Christendom.* Jim, the main character, has just heard the radio announcement of England's declaration of war on Germany in 1939:

> "That means we've declared war. Did you hear that, Dad? We've declared war."
>
> "'Bout time, too," said his father roundly. "Folks was beginning to wonder if they meant to."

But it was easy for him. He was old. He didn't have to turn around and look at the thing and find it the only thing in the world. His very self would endure and would not be changed. The responsibility was not his, the terror was not his. If there should be a vision, the vision would not be his, and that was gain as well as loss. To be an old man at war, with the weight of life behind you and little need to do anything about anything, that was an easy thing. But to have the whole of life ahead of you, and to have the earth reeling under your feet and the sky bowing over your head, and to feel fallen on your sole self the onus of keeping the one secure and the other suspended, that was not so easy.

He didn't think of it like that. He thought, *I'll have to make up my mind what to do. Up to me to do something now.*

Nothing clearer, nothing more complex than that.

Note that Pargeter's narrative voice here is quite distant—"fallen on your sole self the onus" is probably not a phrase that Jim would come up with on his own—and she clearly marks off Jim's conscious thoughts with both thinker attributions and italics. But though the passage isn't in Jim's voice, it clearly conveys his complex state of mind at a critical moment in the story. The language is sophisticated but it is also specific, focused on Jim, and so never goes over the edge into purple. This is the difference between this passage and the Peter Cooper example from the last chapter.

If you have a poetic turn of mind, you can let it out of its cage from time to time. You just need to remember the other principles we've talked about, such as proportion. When you take the time and energy to capture precisely a particular state of mind, make sure it's a state of mind that's worth capturing—a turning point in your main character's life, a moment of realization that defines his or her entire existence. If you expend your literary gifts on a character's passing fancy or fit of pique, your readers are going to feel manipulated and you'll get in the way of your story.

Also, don't try to keep this kind of writing up for very long. Most of your characters won't have these kinds of descriptive gifts, so the longer you sustain them, the longer you keep your readers away from your character's voice. And even if your viewpoint character is a hypersensitive poet, if you try to keep up this sort of artistic description for too long, you create the impression that your character is in a permanent state of epiphany. Even if readers don't find it improbable, they'll find it exhausting.

So how do you get in and out of a more elevated voice? Well, consider the following description of an evening's ride, from a client's submission. The piece has been edited a bit for brevity:

> "Stride, girl," Sally said to Foxy [her horse] as they neared the creek. "Now let me feel the thunder."
> The thrill of the massive animal unhesitatingly leaping over the water then landing gently and evenly to gallop off for more adventure made Sally Dumont want to ride horses forever, especially at twilight. She could spend hours on horseback, talking to the horses, admiring the contradiction of the evergreens burning

orange in the sun's afterglow and the otherwise blue sky cast in pink streaks and swirls in the western horizon. Mostly, though, she loved the feel of the thunder under her, galloping across the lush expanse. Strength with grace, only horses could be both simultaneously, and she lived to be part of it.

The thunder and the ballet on four frail legs, and she could ride them forever over every acre of her perfect world. First Foxy, then Queenie, then Regal, then Princess and all the others. Even when she was cuddled with Peter under the warm blankets, she was still riding her horses, dreaming of sunsets and of saddles and of freest winds whipping through her hair, as they were just at that moment, when the trees and the sky belied their true colors, and when Foxy was perfectly the thunder and the ballet over a world that was as contented and innocent as Sally and the sky.

Dusk had thrown its shadows over Lil' Hallow, as Peter and Sally more casually called their paradise, a fifty-acre horse farm perfectly isolated in northern North Dakota. The fading light had turned the trunks and fuller boughs of the evergreens at the edge of the meadow into shapeless, shadowy shrouds. From these a graceful illusion of nature slowly took form as magically as a deer's shape finally coming to eye as it stands cloaked among the brush.

Into that illusion Sally rode Foxy. Her long straight hair and the horse's long black tail flew in the wind and the horse's momentum stirred. This was freedom. Each stride brought rhythmic clopping of the hooves against the grass. "Atta girl." The reins jingled. The straps of the leather saddle slapped slightly. "Let yourself ride."

But just as the rim of the sun finally faded into the horizon, Sally slowed and turned the horse so that they faced the afterglow. "Our favorite spot."

Foxy neighed softly and threw her head from side to side as if she agreed.

"You're really happy tonight," Sally said, patting the horse's neck. "I know, I know, I love it just as much as you do. I could just die out here—but only if heaven has land like this so we can ride forever. And the sunset, too. And all the other horses. Think it does, girl? Think heaven has a place for horses and riding?"

Foxy neighed again, more loudly, ears twitching.

"I think so too, but that's a long time away."

They were standing in a spotlight on a stage because over them was a bright glow that had descended from some balcony high in the sky, and the spot where the sun might have just set. Behind and around them were the shadows where the audience should have been clapping. Foxy neighed and proudly held her head high, her ears turning and twitching as though she were listening for that applause. The chirruping of crickets could have been that applause and the sea of fireflies, the camera flashes. Each second, the light before them receded further, as though a stagehand were turning away the spotlight and saving it for another performance on another perfect evening, which would no doubt be

tomorrow, and the next day, and the next day—every
day as far as Sally was concerned.

"Can't stay out here forever. Giddyup."

This is not bad, but note that the writer keeps slipping
into and out of the more elevated voice. The second paragraph seems more self-conscious and more in Sally's voice
("She could spend hours on horseback . . ."). But by the end
of the third paragraph the language has clearly pulled away
from anything she might express consciously—few people
think of themselves as "contented and innocent . . . as the
sky." The exposition on the name of the farm is an intrusive
bit of self-consciousness, as is her conversation with Foxy,
and the final metaphor, of the spotlight and the camera
flashes, is somewhere in between. She might be consciously
aware of the resemblance or she might simply feel as if she
were onstage without articulating it to herself.

Of course, it's possible that Sally did keep dropping into
and out of the state of wordless joy that the elevated language captures, and if that's the writer's intent, then well and
good. But it takes readers time to move into and out of this
emotional state, so jumping back and forth too quickly can
leave them behind. Now take a look at the edited version:

"Stride, girl," Sally said to Foxy as they neared the
creek.

The massive animal leapt over the water and landed
gently and evenly to gallop off for more adventure and
Sally Dumont wanted to ride horses forever, especially

at twilight. She could spend hours on horseback with Foxy, then Queenie, then Regal, then Princess then around again in turn. Talking to them, admiring the contradiction of the evergreens burning orange in the sun's afterglow while the otherwise blue sky was cast in pink streaks and swirls in the western horizon overhead. Mostly, though, she loved the thunder under her.

Strength with grace, thunder and ballet on four frail legs. Only horses could be both simultaneously, and she could ride them forever over every acre of her perfect world. Even when she was cuddled with Peter under the warm blankets, she was still riding her horses, dreaming of sunsets and saddles and freest winds whipping through her hair, as they were just at that moment, when the trees and the sky belied their true colors, and when Foxy was perfectly the thunder and the ballet over a world that was as contented and innocent as Sally and the sky.

Dusk had thrown its shadows over Lil' Hallow. The fading light had turned the trunks and fuller boughs of the evergreens at the edge of the meadow into shapeless, shadowy shrouds. From these a graceful illusion of nature slowly took form as magically as a deer's shape finally coming to eye as it stands cloaked among the brush.

Into that illusion Sally rode Foxy. Her long straight hair and the horse's long black tail flew in the wind and the horse's momentum stirred.

Then, just as the rim of the sun finally faded into the horizon, Sally slowed and turned the horse so that they faced the afterglow, standing in a spotlight on stage as a bright beam descended from some balcony high in the sky. Behind and around them were the shadows where the audience should have been clapping. Foxy neighed and proudly held her head high, her ears turning and twitching as though she were listening for that applause. The chirruping of crickets could have been that applause and the sea of fireflies, the camera flashes. Each second, the light before them receded further, as though a stagehand were turning away the spotlight and saving it for another performance on another perfect evening, which would no doubt be tomorrow, and the next day, and the next day—every day as far as Sally was concerned.

Foxy neighed softly and threw her head from side to side.

Sally patted the horse's neck. "I know, I know, I love it just as much as you do. I could just die out here—but only if heaven has land like this so we can ride forever. And the sunset, too. And all the other horses. Think it does, girl? Think heaven has a place for horses and riding?"

Foxy neighed again, more loudly, ears twitching.

"I think so too, but that's a long time away. Well, can't stay out here forever. Giddyup."

Note that we saved the thunder metaphor until Sally is immersed in wordless joy and used the (more self-conscious) theater metaphor to show that she's coming down from it. The exposition is gone, and the conversation with the horse is moved to the end, when she's turned her mind back to practical matters, like getting home before dark. Using this kind of elevated language to capture a mood your character wouldn't describe—at least not at the moment he or she is experiencing it—is a delicate matter. You need to be gentle and sparing to make it work.

Also, remember that even those writers with the most distinctive voices did not develop those voices overnight. Melville simply couldn't have written *Omoo* in the voice he used in *Moby-Dick.* He just wasn't ready yet. In order to write with a mature voice, you have to mature first.

But though you shouldn't consciously work on your voice as you write, there is a way to encourage it when you get to the self-editing stage. Start by rereading a short story, scene, or chapter as if you were reading it for the first time (rather as you would read in self-editing for proportion). Whenever you come to a sentence or phrase that gives you a little jab of pleasure, that makes you say, "Ah, yes," that *sings*—highlight that passage in a color you like (we use yellow) or underline it. Then go through and read aloud all the sentences you highlighted or underlined. Don't analyze them for the moment, just try to absorb their rhythm or fullness or simplicity or freshness or whatever made them sing to you. What you've been reading aloud will represent, for now, your voice at its most effective. And making yourself conscious of it in this mechanical way will strengthen it as you continue your work.

Now read through the same section again, and when you

come to those passages that make you wince or that seem to fall flat, just draw a wavy line under them. Go back and read consecutively all the passages you didn't like, and this time try to analyze what makes them different from the passages that sang to you. *Is* the writing flat? Strained? Awkward? Obvious? Pedestrian? Forced? Vague or abstract?

If flatness seems to be the problem, take a look at the surrounding sentences and see if they don't all have the same structure. Too many straight declarative sentences in a row, for instance, will flatten out anyone's writing. If the problem is abstraction or vagueness, rewrite for specificity. "A man walked into the room and ordered a drink" hasn't one fifth the bite of "A dwarf stepped up to the bar and ordered a Bloody Mary."

If the passage seems obvious, check for explanations— whether in dialogue, interior monologue, even narration— and cut or rewrite accordingly. And if the writing seems strained or forced or awkward, try reading the passage aloud, listening carefully for any little changes you're inclined to make while reading. More often than not, those changes will be in the direction of your natural voice.

If you do this exercise often enough, you will develop a sensitivity to your own voice that will gently encourage the development of the confidence and distinction you're after. And this is as true of character voice as it is of narrative voice. If you don't pay meticulous attention to the people you're writing about, their voices can seem interchangeable.

In the passages that follow, taken from *The Company of Women,* Mary Gordon gives us first-person narration from each major character in the novel up to that point:

It was because of the bats that I decided to marry.

The attic of our house was infested with bats. And yet we carefully avoided mentioning anything, out of some fairy-tale logic, for we knew that the first to speak would have to be the first to act. Cyprian was in the hospital. We were afraid he was dying. We were alone; we were women. We decided to be silent. Except my daughter, Linda. Daily, not less than three times a day for a week, she would say, "Something stinks in here." It was not I who taught her that diction. [Felicitas]

The loss of Cyprian will be terrible, but I know about loss, and I no longer fear it. What I fear is that the center will not hold, that without him we will lose ourselves, that Felicitas and Leo will move off the land, and Clare will decide that life here is too dull for her, and Charlotte will stay with me reluctantly, out of duty. This is the proof of selfish nature: I see the death of a man I have loved for forty years, who has guided my soul, who has kept me from terror and held back despair—I see his death in terms of the breakup of the neighborhood. [Charlotte]

Apart from him, I belong to no one; no one is fond of me except perhaps the child, and she would forget me in an hour. I must be seen, after he dies, as a burden, an unpaid debt.

So I am condemned to stay with them, homeless in my own home, suffered, borne, worse than a poor relation, for I am tied by no blood. There is nothing to bind me to them, only Cyprian, who has decided to die, leaving us to one another. [Muriel]

I fear the clips and stings of other human lives, lives less careful than my own. I fear the sound of Muriel's voice, the print of her green curtains; I fear Elizabeth's clumsiness and her uncertainties, Felicitas' rudeness and judgments; the ill-timed demands of Linda, the physical weakness of Cyprian . . . I fear they will think my house is their house, that they can come in any time, sit anywhere, use anything. I am taking a risk, but in old age risk may be the only wise investment. [Clare]

I have had to learn the discipline of prosperous love, I have had to be struck down by age and sickness to feel the great richness of the ardent, the extraordinary love I live among. I have had to learn ordinary happiness, and from ordinary happiness, the first real peace of my life, my life which I had wanted full of splendor. . . . Now every morning is miraculous to me. I wake and see in the thin, early light the faces of my friends. [Cyprian]

Everyone is old here but my mother and me. All the people my mother loves are old but me. Soon they will die. That's why my mother wants to marry Leo. So that all the people she loves will not be old and dying . . .

Now I see my mother leaning on her shovel; now I see my grandmother. They are laughing and they see me at the window. "Come out," they say, "come out and talk to us. We're lonely for you. Tell us something." [Linda]

Every voice is distinct, because each one belongs to a character with a distinct personality and sensibility—this despite the fact that all of the characters are Catholics and most of them are elderly women with the same educational background. Every voice seems to arise spontaneously from the character rather than the writer; nothing about the voices seems forced or unnatural.

Why? We doubt very much that it's because Mary Gordon sat down beforehand and worked out six different styles of speech and thought for six different characters. What's far more likely is that she has listened to her characters, has come to know them so intimately that one of them *can't* speak in the same voice as another.

"The limitation of the great stylists—Henry James, say, or Hemingway," writes Frederick Buechner in the essay collection *Spiritual Quests,* "is that you remember their voices long after you've forgotten the voices of any of the people they wrote about. In one of the Psalms, God says, 'Be still and know that I am God.' I've always taken that to be good literary advice, too. Be still the way Tolstoy is still, be still the way Anthony Trollope is still, so that your characters can become gods and speak for themselves and come alive in their own way."

In chapter 6, we suggested reading aloud, consecutively, the dialogue of each major character to encourage your distinguishing their voices. Well, reading aloud consecutively all the passages written from each major character's point of view can help you spot any places where a character's voice doesn't fit the character. Listen to what each one in turn says or thinks, and let your ear come up with the correction for anything that rings false to that character, any line of dialogue or thought that doesn't sound like what he or she would say or think. Very often a character's voice will develop as much or more in the revision process as in the first draft.

And that's true for voice overall, as well. The greatest advantage of self-editing—including the highlighting we've recommended in this chapter—is the kind of attention you have to pay to your own work while you're doing the self-editing. It demands that you revise again and again until what you've written rings true. Until you can believe it.

It invites you to listen to your work. Do that job of listening carefully enough, lovingly enough, and you will start to hear your own writing voice.

Checklist and Exercises

Realistically, we can't really come up with a list of things to watch for as you improve your voice—there are no rules to becoming an individual. And the best exercise in developing your voice is to work on your own manuscript.

So go to it, and good luck.

ANSWERS
TO EXERCISES

Actually, "answers" is a misnomer, since literature is not so much correct (or incorrect) as it is effective (or ineffective). You will have edited the exercises we've given you differently and in some cases more effectively than we have. Still, you might find it helpful to see what we've come up with.

Chapter 1

A.   *A fairly simple one to start with. The writer breaks into the middle of a conversation to summarize one of the responses for us. Convert that bit of narrative summary into dialogue, and the scene works much better.*

"Mortimer? Mortimer?" Simon Hedges said. "Where are you?"

"Look up, you ninny. I'm on the roof."

"What in blue blazes are you doing perched up there?"

"The cupola and weather vane finally got here," Mortimer said. "I couldn't wait all day for you to install the gadgets, so here I am."

"How's it going so far?"

"I'm still sorting through the directions."

"Well, come on down before you kill yourself," Simon said. "I swear I'll put them up for you this afternoon."

B.   *A slightly different approach to showing and telling. Rather than simply describing the effect the shop had on the narrator, describe the shop itself and let it have the same effect on the reader. As in:*

I always figured I knew Uncle Zeb, until the day I walked into his shop.

It was a small room, not much bigger than most kitchens. But it was packed full of junk. No, not junk, junk isn't that well organized. *Stuff.* Two of the walls were covered floor to ceiling with those metal shelves you see in library basements, and those shelves were full of neat little boxes with labels like "Bearings and Races" or "Angle Brackets, ⅜ and Larger."

And the tools! There was a drill press in one

corner next to the metal shelves and a lathe along the opposite wall. And a pegboard up above the workbench with two rows—two whole rows—of screwdrivers. There was a row of hammers—huge ones with big flat heads and little bitty ones with pointy heads, and some made out of rubber and some of lead. There were twenty-one different pairs of pliers (I counted), from big thick ones about a foot long to tiny things that were almost tweezers. There were tools I couldn't even recognize, things that had been made to do just one job and do it perfectly.

These weren't a handy guy's tools. A handy guy can keep all his tools in a drawer or in a box in the garage. No. These belonged to a craftsman.

C.   *Of course, no two versions of this exercise are going to look alike. Here's our take on the piece:*

Roger realized he'd made a mistake about five minutes after he tried the shortcut off of 9W. He'd been through about six intersections, and none of them had met at right angles.

He stopped to read a sign by the light of a streetlamp. Terpsichore Terrace. He didn't think he'd seen that one before, so he took a left.

Two lefts (Xanadu Drive, Lenape Lane), a right (Camelot Court), and a few long, gentle curves later, he was back on Terpsichore Terrace. He couldn't be at the intersection he'd started at—he'd come too far for that. But the Blessed Virgin under the upturned bathtub in front of him did look familiar.

No, the other one had marigolds in front of it, and this one had . . . well . . . something else.

He pounded the steering wheel. All he wanted was a *street*. Something called "road" or "route," or even "avenue." Something with yellow lines down the middle. Something that went somewhere.

He parked, walked up to the Blessed Virgin's house and knocked. At least he could hope for a Christian reception.

"Sorry to bother you this late, but I seem to be a little twisted around. Can you tell me how to find 9W?"

"Of course. Let me see." The man stepped onto the porch and peered into the night. "What you want to do is turn around, then follow this road, Terpsichore Terrace, until it becomes Belleville Drive. Then you would take the . . . let me see . . ." He began to tick them off on his fingers. "The fourth right—I can't recall the name of the street right now. Then the first left and follow that road until it ends."

Roger pointed. "This way until Belleville, fourth right, first left, follow to the end."

"That's all there is to it."

"Thanks."

Twenty minutes later Roger was facing a small, square house with a cast-iron deer in the front yard. On Xanadu Drive. Doubtless just a stone's throw from Terpsichore Terrace. He walked to the front door and pounded.

"Yeah?" Not elderly, balding, T-shirt, no cardigan.

"Can I use your phone?"

"Yeah, sure."

Ten minutes later, the taxi pulled up behind his car. "What happened, Mac, you break down?"

"No, but I'm on the verge. I just want you to lead me back to 9W."

"No problem. 9W's about six bucks from here."

Roger paid the money gladly. "You don't seem surprised."

"Why should I be? You're the third one so far this year."

Chapter 2

A.   *Exactly how you would convey Maggie's character through scenes depends, of course, on the plot of your story. You could show her lack of kinship with anybody but her own age group by giving her a linguistic quirk, some bit of slang or unusual phraseology that is shared by her friends and mystifying to everyone else.*

And if your plot would allow it, there is real dramatic potential in revealing her character a little at a time. The beginning of the story could show only the more comic (and typical) aspects of her character—the restless energy, the boredom with everyone around her, the supercharged thoughts. Then, as the plot develops, you could start to show the fears behind the boredom, perhaps even including some hints of desperation. In short, you could turn Maggie into a real human being.

B. *Again, the details of how to show the changes in the county depend on the details of your plot. One good approach would be to use the changes to the county as a backdrop for the story. For instance, you could have Fred get lost on his way to, say, his old high school because some of the roads he used then have become one-way. Or you could give him an occasional flashback to one of the family farms he remembers. Or you could simply have him express his disgust at the state of Route 59 to one of the other characters.*

Chapter 3

A. *Okay, an easy one. The point of view essentially alternates between Ed and Susan. The first paragraph is clearly Susan's point of view, since it contains her interior monologue. The third is from Ed's (same* *reason). "They had no time to lose" is practically omniscient narrator. When Susan is in the living room, she can't see Ed dashing around the kitchen. And after Ed ducks through the back door, he can't see Susan and the realtor's clients come in from the living room.*

If you were to break the action up into different scenes separated by linespaces (as we did with the Harley example), each scene would only be a paragraph or so long. Since that's a bit short for a scene, a better approach might be to write everything from either Ed or Susan's point of view, or to have at most one break in mid-scene. You probably wouldn't want to use the omniscient narrator. You want your readers to feel the panic along with Ed and Susan, and the omniscient narrator would be too distracting.

So the answer is to pick one point of view or the other and stick with it. Perhaps Susan could hear Ed clanking around in the kitchen while she power-straightens the living room. Or perhaps Ed could hear Susan trying to lead the realtor upstairs as he ducks out the back door.

B.   *Here, the point of view shifts are more subtle. For one thing, Lance would be unlikely to think of a New York cab as a "New York cab," especially if he was a native New Yorker. And from his point of view, he didn't disappear into the crowd.*

C.   *Let's try the first person first, writing from inside the head of an eight-year-old.*

SELF-EDITING FOR FICTION WRITERS

Miss Tessmacher was up at the board talking about subtraction or something. She'd just given us her pay-attention-you'll-need-this-when-you-grow-up lecture, so she wouldn't look this way for a while yet. Across the aisle, Sandy Dwerkin was working on a note to pass to Edith-the-Hog Hoagland. I was leafing through my English reader looking for some picture I maybe hadn't seen yet, when I happened to look out the window.

Snow!

All of a sudden, it was hard to sit still.

It was just a few little tiny flakes spitting down from the clouds and they wouldn't close the schools for it and it probably wouldn't even stick. But, jeez, it was only October and we were getting snow already. And maybe it *would* stick, it had been pretty cold lately, and the clouds looked serious—black and thick like they were going to be there a while.

Just until dismissal. Just through the rest of math and then English and then story time, that's all. If it would just keep snowing until then, everything would be perfect.

Gosh, snow already!

Now let's try it from the omniscient. Since we're no longer limited to Mitch's perspective on life, we can make the narrative voice a bit more mature, even world-weary.

Of all the long and arbitrary divisions of the school day, fifth period is probably the hardest. Recess and lunch, along with the little bit of anticipation and excitement they can generate, are long since over. Dismissal is still two periods away, much too far ahead to even imagine. All that lies before the student, all that lay before Mitch, was the uninterrupted hard work of learning.

So, of course, it was the perfect time for the snow to begin.

The snowfall was hardly substantial, little more than a reminder that winter had arrived and a promise of what was to come. But that was enough to fire Mitch's imagination with pictures of the coming season of sledding, snowball fights, and, best of all, school closings. Though he was not aware of them, there were even hints of Christmas in his anticipation. Those few flakes represented the sea-change of the seasons, with all that it entailed.

Dismissal suddenly became delicious, and the long wait for the final bell all but unendurable.

And once more, from the third person.

Fifth period was always the hardest. Miss Tessmacher, up by the board, droned on about subtraction, Sandy Dwerkin scribbled a note to pass to Edith Hoagland, and Mitch flipped idly through his English book. A subtle motion outside caught the corner of his eye and he looked out the window next to his desk.

Snow!

The snow didn't amount to much—only an occasional spattering of delicate white flakes—but that didn't matter. Even though it was only October, autumn had turned a corner and become winter, with all that winter meant. Sledding, snowball fights with his sister, even school closings, were all right there in those few little flakes. If only it would last until dismissal.

Suddenly he found it hard to sit still.

Chapter 4

A.   *The writer here not only spends too much time on characters we're never going to meet again, he gives us far more detail than an exhausted runner, intent on finishing the race, is likely to notice. All you need is:*

As he approached the last hill, Carter passed another runner who had started fast but was now spent and fading, his once-crisp stride now a weary shuffle.

B. *Here, the problem is too little detail. That glass of water seems to materialize out of nowhere.*

She walked to the sink, reached for a glass, and turned on the tap. "Watch out for the egg."

It was too late. Eddy was wiping his eyes and didn't see it. His foot slipped and he landed on the yolk. He began crying again.

Dotty wanted to join him. She dropped the glass, grabbed him by the arm, and dragged him to the sink, where she tried to wipe his pants with the dishrag.

"Stop crying." She fished the glass out of the sink, refilled it, and handed it to him. "Drink this, then go change your pants."

Chapter 5

A. *A fairly easy one to begin with. Lots of unusual speaker attributions, some repetition, a few -lys. A little too much direct address, more speaker attributions than are strictly needed. And note that the sighing has been converted from a speaker attribution to a beat. Most of the editing was simply cutting, and the results look like this:*

"You aren't seriously thinking about putting that trash in your body, are you?"

I put down the package of Twinkies and turned around. It was Fred McDermot, an acquaintance from work.

"Pardon me," I said.

"You heard me."

I sighed. "Fred, I can't for the life of me see why this is any of your business."

"I'm just thinking of you, that's all," he said. "Do you know what they put in those things?"

"No."

"Neither do I. That's the point."

B.   *Of course, it's a risky business trying to rewrite a classic like* Gatsby. *And some of you will probably feel we have edited some of the character out of the passage, some of the lushness that makes the novel what it is. Well, we do believe there is room for lushness in fiction, but not in the dialogue mechanics. And no matter how much of a genius Fitzgerald may have been, when he writes "he assured us positively," he's not at his best. After all, can you assure someone negatively?*

Here's our re-edit of an American classic:

"I like to come," Lucille said. "I never care what I do, so I always have a good time. When I was here last, I tore my gown on a chair, and he asked me my name and address—within a week I got a package from Croirier's with a new evening gown in it."

"Did you keep it?" Jordan asked.

"Sure I did. I was going to wear it tonight, but it was too big in the bust and had to be altered. It was gas blue with lavender beads. Two hundred and sixty-five dollars."

"There's something funny about a fellow that'll do a thing like that," said the other girl. "He doesn't want any trouble with *any*body."

"Who doesn't?" I said.

"Gatsby. Somebody told me—"

The two girls and Jordan leaned together.

"Somebody told me they thought he killed a man."

A thrill passed over all of us. The three Mr. Mumbles bent forward in their seats.

"I don't think it's so much *that*," Lucille said. "It's more that he was a German spy during the war."

One of the men nodded. "I heard that from a man who knew all about him, grew up with him in Germany."

"Oh no," said the first girl, "it couldn't be that, because he was in the American army during the war." As our credulity switched back to her, she leaned forward. "You look at him sometimes when he thinks nobody's looking at him. I'll bet he killed a man."

Chapter 6

A. *Four sailors shooting the breeze in complete, precise, well-rounded sentences. There were two little speeches, the first paragraph and the next to last, which we broke up with some give and take and by distributing the dialogue among the characters. We got rid of the scare quotes (which we cover in chapter 11), and also threw in a few contractions and one profanity for good measure. As edited, the scene reads:*

As they sat quietly catching their breath, Getz turned to Wheeler. "Kid, we've all been diving together a long time and are real comfortable with each other. You're new. We hear you're good, but you're still new."

"What's your point?"

"You wouldn't object to a question or two, would you?"

"Ask away."

"What's your maximum no-decompress bottom time at three atmospheres?"

"The U.S. Navy tables allow sixty minutes at sixty feet with a standard rate of ascent. How's that?"

"Good enough," Nick said. "Welcome aboard."

"No offense, kid," Getz said. "We're generally more than ten hours from a doctor and there's no recompression chamber in the whole damn country. We can't afford to push the tables."

Lou grinned. "You mean we can't afford to *regularly* push the tables."

B.   *This one is rather like one of those "What's wrong with this picture?" puzzles. You can see there are a lot of problems. The challenge lies in catching them all. As edited, the scene reads like this:*

I peered through the front window of the garage, which did me no good because light hadn't been able to penetrate that window since man landed on the moon.

I tapped on the door. "Anybody here?"

A man came out from the shop wearing greasy, half-unzipped coveralls with the name "Lester" stitched in over the pocket. I hoped he took those off before he got into my car. Lester took his cigar stub out of his mouth and spat near my feet.

"Yeah, what can I do you for?"

"Well, my name is Baumgarten. I'm here to pick up my car. Is it ready?"

"Hang on a sec." He stepped back into the shop and picked up a greasy clipboard with a thick wad of forms under the clip. "What was the name again, Bumgarden?"

"BAUMgarten." You cretin.

"Yeah, right." He pawed through the forms. "Don't see you here, Mr. BAUMgarden. Sorry."

"What do you mean, sorry? You have my car in there. Either it's fixed or it's not."

"Look, mister, what do you think, I got time to get, like, intimate with all my clientele? You could be Baumgarden, you could be his cousin, you could be Governor Pataki for all I know."

"I'd be happy to show you my driver's—"

"It don't matter. I ain't giving you no car unless you got papers and I got matching papers. Far as I'm concerned, you ain't on this clipboard, you don't exist."

Chapter 7

A. *Yes, the mechanics are a mess. But notice how they kept the narrative distance moving from intimate to distant and back again. We've brought a bit more consistency to the passage:*

"Excuse me, miss, but I'm giving a seminar over in room 206 in a few minutes, and I need an overhead projector."

The man at the door of the audiovisual room was actually wearing a tweed jacket with leather patches at the elbows. Typical English professor. All he needed was a pipe.

"Okay," Kimberly said, "if you want an overhead or something like that—a movie projector or slides or whatever—you have to fill out a form ahead of time. Then we can, like, line everything up and—"

"I know. I sent in the form three weeks ago."

"You've been up to the seminar room?"

"Yes, and the projector wasn't there."

Okay, great. She'd only taken over from Ed yesterday, and here was her first major screw-up. "Okay, do you have your, what do you call it, your course form?"

He snapped his briefcase open and pulled out the familiar green card. "Right here."

"Yeah, give me a minute."

She ducked into the office and dug out the clipboard with all the requisitions on it. A few minutes later, the guy stuck his head in the office.

"Miss?" he said. "I don't want to be late."

"What's the course number?"

"A3205."

She went through the forms again. Definitely no A3205 there. "What's the room number?"

"As I believe I just told you, it's 206. I don't suppose you could just give me a projector now, could you? I'd be happy to carry it over myself."

"Nope, we don't have any to spare. If you want

one, we have to figure out where yours went." One more time through the forms, and there it was. "Okay, here's the problem. I have room 206 listed as A9631, 'Making Fresh Baby Food at Home.' The projector should be up there."

"Miss, the projector's not there," he said. "That's why I'm here."

Jeez, what did it take to please this guy? "You're sure? Did you check the closet?"

"Room 206 doesn't have a closet."

"Sure it does. It's the big seminar room off the cafeteria, right?"

"No, it's a smallish room near the elevators. How long have you worked here?"

"Long enough to know the building. Did you come across the courtyard to get here?"

"Um, yes, I did."

"Okay, we don't handle that wing of the building. You want the AV room for the Peebles annex; it's down by the bursar's office."

"Oh, I see." He looked at his watch. "Well, thank you."

"Hey, no sweat. We're here to serve."

B.   *We've made the language more idiomatic ("Hadn't been" rather than "There had been no") and the choice of details more personal (Winston probably wouldn't think of the name of the road he walked every morning).*

Hadn't been rain for coming on two weeks, and the leaves crunched underfoot. Winston would have to get the hose out of the basement when he got home, get some water on the garden. He stepped out into Dymond's land and stopped. Was that wood smoke? It was too warm for anyone to be using a stove. Brush fire? Or had the neighbors started a brush burn without a permit again?

C. *Again, we're editing some brilliant writers, which is a little risky. But then, the better the writers, the more they deserve careful editing. So here's our take on three modern masters:*

"You see," Smiley said, "our obsession with virtue won't go away. Self-interest is so *limiting*. So is expediency." He paused again, still deep inside his own thoughts. "All I'm really saying, I suppose, is that if the temptation to humanity does assail you now and then, I hope you won't take it as a weakness in yourselves, but give it a fair hearing."

Of course. The cufflinks. George was remembering the old man.

—JOHN LE CARRÉ, *The Secret Pilgrim*

"Did you go up there? When you were young?"

"I went to dances," the doctor said. "I specialized in getting Cokes for people. I was extremely good at getting Cokes passed around."

He helped her into a chair. "Now, then, what can I do for you?"

Amanda sat her pocketbook down on the floor and told him what she had come for.

Jesus Christ. How many years would he have to practice medicine before he learned never to be surprised at anything?

—ELLEN GILCHRIST, *The Annunciation*

This wasn't Dalgliesh's case and he couldn't stop Mair by force. But at least he could ensure that the direct path to the body lay undisturbed. Without another word he led the way and Mair followed. But . . . why this insistence on seeing the body? To satisfy himself that she was, in fact, dead, the scientists' need to verify and confirm? Or was he trying to exorcise a horror he knew could be more terrible in imagination than in reality? Or was there, perhaps, a deeper compulsion, the need to pay her the tribute of standing over her body in the quietness and loneliness of the night before the police arrived with all the official paraphernalia of a murder investigation to violate forever the intimacies they had shared?

—P. D. JAMES, *A Taste for Death*

Chapter 8

A. *At least one beat between every line of dialogue, some of them clichés (kicking the tire, for instance) and some of them simply too detailed (three separate actions to open the hood). Try the scene again with the deadwood gone.*

"You're sure it runs?" Mr. Dietz said.

I leaned against the fender. "It did last time I tried it."

"Yeah, well, when was that?"

"Just last week. Here, listen."

I hopped in the front seat and hit the starter. The engine caught, then sputtered and died. I pumped the gas once or twice and tried again. This time it caught and began to purr.

"Well, I don't know. It sounds all right, but I don't like the looks of the body." He kicked the fender, and little flakes of rust fluttered to the ground.

"Look, for three hundred dollars, what do you want?" I revved it a little. "I mean, listen to that, it's running like a baby. You should get twenty thousand miles out of this with no trouble. At least twenty."

He peered into one of the wheel wells. "As long as one of the tires doesn't fall off on me."

"There's a spare in the trunk. Now what do you say?"

B. *Now for one where you have to put the beats in. In this particular example, the beats help add a sense of rhythm to the dialogue, to show some of the hesitance that can come with strong emotion.*

"Do you really think this is a smart move?" she said. "I mean, you don't know anybody in California."

"I'm pretty sure." She could see him lying there in the moonlight, hands behind his head, staring at the ceiling. "After all, it's not as if I have a choice. You've got to go where the jobs are."

"What about the kids?"

He rolled to face her. "Honey, it's not like I'm going to be gone forever. I'll send for you as soon as I can."

"Yeah, but when will that be? Where are you going to stay, what are you going to do, how are you going to live there?"

"I'm taking the tent, and I can sleep in the car if need be. Besides, I'll find something within a week, I'll bet you."

"I . . ." Her hands were knotted in the sheet. She forced herself to let go. "It's just that I'm scared."

He reached out to her and brushed back a wisp of hair that had fallen over one eye. "I know. So am I."

Chapter 9

A.   *Of course, a written piece is different from a radio monologue, and the central character is a Lake Wobegonian. But we still felt this needed a bit more drive.*

It has been a quiet week in Lake Wobegon. Sunday morning Clarence Bunsen stepped into the shower and turned on the water—which was cold, but he's Norwegian, he knows you have to take what you get—and stood until it got warm, and he was reaching for the soap when he thought for sure he was having a heart attack. He'd read a *Reader's Digest* story about a man's heart attack ("My Most Unforgettable Experience") and this felt like the one in the story—chest pain like a steel band tightening.

Clarence grabbed the nozzle as the rest of the story flashed before his eyes: the ride in the ambulance, the dash to the emergency room, unconsciousness as the heart team worked over him, the long slow recovery and the discovery of a new set of values.

But as he imagined what was about to happen, the heart attack petered out on him. The story said it felt like an elephant stepping on you. This felt more like a big dog, and then somebody whistled and the dog left.

So it wasn't a heart attack, there was no story, and Clarence felt better.

B. *New paragraphs for new speakers, trim back on the beats a little, and break up the longer speeches with some give-and-take or by running two sentences together into one.*

Jeanine stared at the spider plant hung over the kitchen sink. Most of its leaves were yellow and a few were going brown at the edges.

"I don't believe this," she said.

"What?" Ed said.

"I only gave you this plant a month ago, and look at it now." She reached out and tenderly touched one of the leaves. It came off in her hand. "I mean, this is a spider plant. They thrive on neglect. How did you manage to do this much damage so quickly?"

"I don't know. I've been watering it once a week, just like you said, I've even been using plant food I picked up at the hardware store the other day."

"What kind of plant food?"

"It's that blue powder that dissolves in water, one tablespoon to the quart."

One tablespoon? "Ed, let me see that plant food."

He opened the cupboard under the sink,

rummaged for a moment, and came up with a box with a picture on the front. She took it and scanned the instructions.

"According to this, you're supposed to use one teaspoon to the quart."

"Oh, well, I guess that explains it, then."

Chapter 10

A.   *A funny idea undone by overkill. With a little less detail on the social graces of a bachelor's apartment, the scene works much better. Also, notice that we've changed the velvet couch to satin, just to get rid of the repetition of "velvet."*

"Come on in, don't be bashful."

It wasn't exactly bashfulness that was keeping me in the hallway. This was my first visit to a bachelor's apartment, and I was shocked at how much it lived up to the reputation.

It wasn't just the velvet painting of Elvis on the wall above the blue satin couch, or the orange shag rug, or even the brown recliner with the cigarette burns in front of the TV. It was the unidentified stains on the ceiling that made me wonder. Those and the nicks in the top of the Formica coffee table that looked as if they might have been caused by tap shoes. Also the TV antenna was a bent coat hanger with an undershirt hanging from it, presumably a dirty undershirt, though I didn't want to get close enough to check.

"Like it?" he said. "I spent all day yesterday cleaning it up, just for you."

B. *Again, we need to hear something of Clancy, but the writer tells us how boring he is once or twice too often—especially considering that he's a minor character we don't meet again. As edited, the passage reads:*

Clancy is a referral from Marilyn Reinhold via Donald Grayson via Rose Sumner. It doesn't speak well for my colleagues, passing the man around that way, not that I blame them. There are so many interesting people in this city who get into therapy—trisexual television producers, addicted actresses, ad agency workaholics, manic-depressive Wall Street dynamos—that it hardly seems necessary to suffer through a patient like Clancy. An accountant for a small rock-salt distributor in Queens, he's a timid man with a nasal, rambling speaking style, so slow you could doze off before he gets the next word out. Usually the words are about his employer of ten years, who pays him at the end of that loyal service the great sum of $42,000 per year, expects overtime without pay, and for some reason has Clancy's undying allegiance. Clancy's really a very nice man, but his problems are small, *small*, and boring.

Chapter 11

A. *Somehow our compunctions about editing a modern master weren't as strong on this one. Here are the results:*

She grabbed up a pelt, pulled it close about her, and gave him an impishly wicked grin. Then she turned on her heels with a low laugh, went to the hearth, and laid small logs upon the still warm coals. She blew on them but drew back in haste when the ashes flew up.

Wulfgar's amused chuckles filled the room. She made a face at him and swung the kettle of water on its hook over the building heat. He crossed to the warmth of the fire beside her and began to dress.

B. *The trick, of course, is to get rid of the unusual speaker attributions and interior monologue mechanics and still preserve the flavor of the original. For what it's worth, here's our version:*

All this time Tweedledee was trying his best to fold up the umbrella with himself in it, which was such an extraordinary thing to do that it quite took off Alice's attention from the angry brother. Tweedledee's attempts ended in his rolling over, bundled up in the umbrella, with only his head out. And there he lay, opening and shutting his mouth and his large eyes, looking more like a fish than anything else.

"Of course you agree to have a battle?" Tweedledum said in a calmer tone.

"I suppose so." The other crawled out of the umbrella. "Only *she* must help us dress up, you know."

So the two brothers went off hand in hand into the wood, and returned in a minute with their arms full of things—bolsters, blankets, hearthrugs, tablecloths, dish covers, and coal scuttles.

"I hope you're a good hand at pinning and tying strings?" Tweedledum said. "Every one of these things has got to go on, somehow or other."

Alice had never seen such a fuss made about anything in all her life—the way those two bustled about, and the quantity of things they put on, and the trouble they gave her in tying strings and fastening buttons. *Really, they'll be more like bundles of old clothes than anything else by the time they're ready.*

"Arrange that bolster round my neck,"
Tweedledee said.

Alice draped the bolster around him as best she
could. "What will this do?"

"Do? Why, it will keep my head from being cut
off, of course. You know, it's one of the most
serious things that can possibly happen to one in a
battle, to get one's head cut off."

C. *Yes, they're all in there. With the description of the
pizza man, we even managed to work a proportion
problem into a single-page exercise.*

"But, Ernestine, honey, I swear I was never
anywhere near the John Smith motel."

"Not according to Helena," Ernestine said.

Winthrop felt like a small boy with a baseball
bat in front of a broken window. A boy who
hadn't broken the window.

"Ernestine, you've got better sense than to listen
to a troublemaking fool like Helena Basquette.
Why only last week—"

The doorbell rang.

Ernestine propped her cigar on the ashtray at
her arm and went to the door.

A tall young man held out a steaming, fragrant
box. "You the guys that ordered the pizza?"

"Winthrop, *sweetie*," Ernestine called over her
shoulder, "are you responsible for this?"

TOP BOOKS
FOR WRITERS

Books on Craft

Block, Lawrence, *Telling Lies for Fun and Profit.* An entertaining nuts-and-bolts book on fiction technique, one of the best. Dialogue section is excellent, particularly helpful on the technique of ellipsis.

Burnett, Hallie, *On Writing the Short Story.* The best book we've found on the subject.

Conrad, Barnaby, *The Complete Guide to Writing Fiction.* Inspiring, helpful essays on theory and technique by the director of the Santa Barbara Writer's Conference and a wide range of well-known fiction craftsmen—from Elmore Leonard to Eudora Welty.

Drury, John, *Creating Poetry.* Thoughtful, knowledgeable, practical advice that helps writers see with the poet's eye. Useful exercises.

Field, Syd, *The Screenwriter's Workbook*. The best hands-on guide we've found, by a veteran who knows his subject and knows how to teach it.

Franklin, Jon, *Writing for Story: Craft Secrets of Dramatic Nonfiction by a Two-Time Pulitzer Prize Winner*. Fiction writers, too, can learn much from this author.

Frey, James, *How to Write a Damn Good Novel*. Helpful emphasis on the three C's of Premise: character, conflict, and conclusion; useful throughout. One of the damn best books on the subject.

Gardner, John, *The Art of Fiction*. Fiction technique and theory—useful, despite the subtitle, for veteran fiction writers as well as novices.

McKee, Robert, *Story: Substance, Structure, Style, and the Principles of Screenwriting*. Written for screenwriters but with principles very applicable to novels.

Stein, Sol, *Stein on Writing*. Perhaps the best book ever written on the overall craft of fiction. Straightforward, practical, easily absorbed.

———, *How to Grow a Novel*. Anecdotal guide to the most common pitfalls in writing a novel and how to avoid them; good tips on honing craft.

Zinsser, William, *On Writing Well: An Informal Guide to Writing Nonfiction*. Despite its title, this superb guide is indispensable to fiction as well as nonfiction writers.

———, *Writing to Learn: How to Write—and Think— Clearly About Any Subject at All* also deserves its classic status.

Books on Inspiration

Goldberg, Bonnie, *Room to Write: Daily Invitations to a Writer's Life.* Two hundred one-page "reusable" assignments that will get the words flowing.

King, Stephen, *On Writing: A Memoir of the Craft.* Part personal story (exceptionally well told, as you might expect), part writing guide, this unusual little book is likely to resonate with many writers. The craft advice is sound, the personal story moving and inspiring.

Lamott, Annie, *Bird by Bird: Some Instructions on Writing and Life.* Hard to describe but wonderful to read. Inspiring, wide-ranging, wise, and entertaining advice for writers in all genres.

Reference Books

Appelbaum, Judith, *How to Get Happily Published.* Still the best book on the subject. Lively, practical, realistic advice and information on everything from agents and editors to book publicity and promotion. Latest edition updated to include advice on electronic media, self-publishing, and so forth.

Bernstein, Theodore M., *The Careful Writer: A Modern Guide to English Usage.* Two thousand alphabetized entries covering issues of grammar, punctuation, usage, and the like. Lively and easy to use.

Herman, Jeff, *Writer's Guide to Book Editors, Publishers, and Literary Agents: Who They Are! What They Want! and How to Win Them Over.* Excellent insider's advice.

Strunk, William, and E. B. White, *The Elements of Style.* The timeless guide to clear and concise usage, now updated by Roger Angell. Still a graceful example of the prose clarity it espouses.

INDEX

Ackroyd, Peter
  Dickens: Life and Times, 18–19
acquisitions editors, 2
action
  as and *-ing* construction and, 193,
    194–95, 208
  in dependent clauses, 192–96
  detail overload effects on, 67–68, 147
  dialogue and, 8, 146
  ellipse bridges for, 68–69
  narrative distance and, 51–52
  repetitive, 14–15
  verb choice and, 89
  See also beats
Adam Dalgleish mysteries (James),
    73–74, 139
Adams, Douglas, 44
adverbs
  as dialogue explanations, 12, 86–88,
    91, 94–95, 141
  sophisticated effects and, 197–99, 208
Airframe (Crichton), 70–71
Alice in Wonderland (Carroll), 162,
    261–63
  stylistic conventions and, 209–11
amateur writing giveaways, 9–10, 89, 219
Animal Dreams (Kingsolver), 151–52
Annunciation, The (Gilchrist), 138–39,
    154–55, 253–54
as construction, 193–95, 208
As I Lay Dying (Faulkner), 219
Astaire, Fred, 208
atmosphere, 73–74
attributions. *See* speaker attributions;
    thinker attributions
authorial voice. *See* voice

balance. *See* proportion
Ballad of Frankie Silver, The
    (McCrumb), 42

beats, 140–59
  balanced use of, 148–49
  characters and, 8, 29, 143, 151–52,
    158
  checklist, 157–58
  choice of, 151–52
  definition of, 8, 29, 143
  dialogue mechanics and, 85, 92, 93,
    95, 141–59
  emotions portrayal through, 144,
    150, 154–55
  exercises, 158–59
  exercises' answers, 255–56
  good examples of, 152–57
  guidelines, 149–52
  observation and, 152
  pitfalls in use of, 144–48, 152
  rhythm and, 149–51, 158
  tension and, 153–57
  uses of, 8, 144, 146, 149, 152
Best Revenge, The (Stein), 43
Billy Bathgate (Doctorow), 199
Billy Shakes (Cooper), 203–4, 221
Black Mountain Breakdown (Smith),
    78–79
blue-pencil editing tradition, 2
Bluest Eye, The (Morrison), 147–48
Bourne Ultimatum, The (Ludlum), 82
brand names
  repetitious use of, 179–80
Brontë, Emily
  Wuthering Heights, 215–16
Buechner, Frederick
  Spiritual Quests, 232
  Treasure Hunt, 153, 167–68
Burroughs, William, 218
Busch, Frederick, 18–19

cadence, 110
Callender, Newgate, 82

Carroll, Lewis
  Alice in Wonderland, 162, 209–11,
    261–63
cartoons
  characters as, 186, 189
chapters
  length and rhythm of, 171, 172
  needless repetition and, 184, 189
characterization, 23–39
  by another character, 29
  atmosphere and, 73–74
  beats and, 146–47, 158
  brand names used for, 179–80
  checklist, 37–38
  cliché avoidance in, 196–97
  dialogue as, 83, 86, 100–108,
    151–52
  exercises, 38–39
  exercises' answers, 239–40
  formulaic, 187
  gradual establishment of, 28–30
  interior monologue and, 33, 117–18
  narrative summary and, 23–26
  personality traits as, 25
  proportion in detail description and,
    77–78
  repetition for, 176
  techniques for, 29–30, 64, 74
characters
  backgrounds of, 26–28
  beats and, 8, 29, 143, 151–52, 158
  as cartoons and stereotypes, 186, 189
  cliché descriptions of, 196–97
  dialogue and, 2, 29, 38, 64, 82–98,
    112
  dialogue attributions and, 88–93
  dialogue give and take between,
    167–68, 172
  dialogue's sound and, 99–115
  different first-person voices of, 43,
    229–32
  distinctive authorial voice and, 218
  distinctive voices of, 232–33
  elevated language and, 202–4,
    219–20, 221–28
  emotions of, 1–2, 16, 50, 51, 57–59,
    64, 116–17, 144
  establishment of, 28–30, 50
  first-person voice and, 41–43, 229–32
  history portrayal of, 24, 26–28, 37, 50

  imagery use by, 202–4, 208
  intimate point of view and, 50
  introduction of, 24–28, 37
  limiting number of, 25–26
  minor, 52, 197
  omniscient voice and, 46
  physical descriptions of, 24–25
  portrayal of thoughts of. *See* interior
    monologue
  profanity use by, 206
  proportion and, 72–74, 77–79, 80
  relationships between, 29
  repetition overkill and, 184, 186–87
  second references to, 91, 95
  taking over story from, 203
  third-person voice discrepancy with,
    48
  viewpoint of, 29–30, 43, 48–66, 68,
    77, 80, 91–92, 229–32
  voice of, 48, 214–15, 221–28,
    232–33
  See also point of view
Christie, Agatha
  Murder at the Vicarage, 76
Chronicle of a Death Foretold (García
    Márquez), 88
Chute, Carolyn
  Letourneau's Used Auto Parts, 49
clichés, 196–97
Colwin, Laurie
  Happy All the Time, 182
commas
  connecting dialogue sentences, 103
  connecting short sentences, 199,
    208
Company of Women, The (Gordon), 43,
    200–202, 229–32
Constant Gardener, The (le Carré),
    216–18
continuity, 13–14
contractions
  in dialogue, 101, 112
Cooper, James Fenimore
  Leatherstocking novels, 188
Cooper, Peter
  Billy Shakes, 203–4, 221
Cottle, Catherine
  The Price of Milk and Money, 111
Crichton, Michael
  Airframe, 70–71

cultures
    expository introduction of, 35–37
cutting
    proportion and, 71–72, 73, 74

Dalgleish, Adam (fictional character),
    73–74, 139, 254
dashes
    for dialogue interruption, 93–94, 95
dependent clauses, 192–96
descriptions
    of character's personal appearance,
        24–25
    development of story and, 183
    overly detailed, 68–69, 77, 80, 147
    pacing of story and, 51
    reading aloud for rhythm and flow,
        107–8
    sex scenes and, 204–6
    use of characters' emotions in, 50–51,
        64, 202
    use of characters' language in, 50–51,
        227–28
    use of character's point of view in,
        77–78
    use of character's voice in, 222
    uses of beats in, 149, 157
detail
    overuse of, 67–69, 80, 147
    viewpoint character's interest and,
        77–78
Devices and Desires (P. D. James), 73–74
dialect, 109–12
dialogue, 82–98
    action and, 8, 146. See also subhead
        beats below
    adverbial explanations for, 12, 86–88,
        91, 94–95, 141
    artificial naturalness of, 100–101, 106
    attributions. See speaker attributions
    beats and, 85, 92, 93, 95, 141–59
    breaks and interchanges in, 167, 172
    characterization through, 29, 38, 83,
        86, 100–108, 151–52
    characters and, 2, 29, 38, 64, 82–98,
        83, 112, 167–68, 172
    checklist, 94–95
    comma usage in, 103
    contraction use in, 101, 112
    creaky mechanics of, 83, 84–85

dash usage in, 93–94, 95
dialect use in, 109–12
distinctive voice and, 218
emotions conveyed by, 64, 83, 84,
    86–87, 116, 150, 202
exercises, 96–98
exercises' answers, 245–47
explanation pitfalls for, 16, 20,
    83–88, 91, 94, 112, 141
exposition in, 31–32, 103, 112
formality avoidance in, 100–104,
    106–7, 167
give and take in, 167–68
interior monologue interruptions in,
    118, 121–22
internal, 127, 128
-ly adverb avoidance, 86–88, 91,
    94–95, 112, 141
misdirection in, 104–5
pace variation in, 144
paragraphing and, 94, 95, 162, 163,
    167–68
polysyllabic words and, 103–4
profanity and, 206, 208
punctuation of, 93–94, 102, 103, 199
reading aloud, 107–9, 112, 151
repetition in, 180
rhythm of, 107, 110, 149–51, 158
sentence fragments in, 101–2
showing vs. telling, 85
sophisticated effects in, 199
stilted, 103
uninterrupted, 147–48
voice and, 107–8
word choice in, 103–4, 110, 112
dialogue, sound of, 99–115
    checklist, 112–13
    exercises, 113–15
    exercises' answers, 248–50
    natural speech techniques and,
        101–12
dialogue mechanics. See dialogue
Dickens: Life and Times (Ackroyd),
    18–19
digressions, 70, 74, 75
Dinner at the Homesick Restaurant
    (Tyler)
    beats and, 155–57
    paragraphing and, 169–71
direct address, 92

distance. *See* narrative distance

distinctive voice, 218–19, 228

Divine Inspiration (Langton), 44–46

Doctorow, E. L.
  Billy Bathgate, 199

Dogsbody (Jones), 35–37

Dorf, Fran
  Flight, 76–77
  Reasonable Madness, A, 140–43, 146, 148, 190–91

Down Will Come Baby (Murphy), 166–67

Dreamcatcher (King), 149–50

Dr. Rocksinger and the Age of Longing (Robinson), 144–45

ear
  dialogue and, 107–8
  exercises, 113–15
  exercises' answers, 248–50
  See also reading aloud

editing, 2–3
  cutting effects on proportion, 71–72, 73, 74
  dialogue and, 82–83
  fresh-eyed manuscript review and, 1, 74–75, 176
  reading passages aloud and, 107–9, 112, 151, 228, 232–33
  for repetition, 188–89
  writing vs., 3–4
  See also manuscripts

effects
  one-time only, 185
  pitfalls of repetition of, 175–76, 177–79
  reasons for repetition of, 182
  sex scenes and, 206
  sophistication and, 193–212

effortless writing
  achievement of, 207–8

Eighth Champion of Christendom, The (Pargeter), 220–21

elevated language, 202–4
  voice and, 219–20, 221–28

Eliot, George
  Middlemarch, 43–44

ellipses
  as action bridgers, 68–69
  dashes in dialogues vs., 93–94, 95

emotions, 20, 116–17
  balanced presentation of, 1–2
  beats as device in portraying, 144, 150, 154–55
  characters and, 1–2, 16, 50, 51, 57–59, 64, 116–17, 144
  dialogue conveying, 64, 83, 84, 86–87, 116, 150, 202
  interior monologues and, 57, 64, 116–17
  narrative intimacy and, 50, 51
  pitfalls of explaining, 84, 95
  point of view and, 57–59
  proportion and, 1–2
  of readers, 10
  showing vs. describing, 16, 17, 20, 87

emphasis quotation marks, 200

engaging the reader, 8–9, 10, 19, 219

exclamation points
  usage avoidance, 200–202, 208

explanations
  pitfalls in dialogue, 16, 20, 83–88, 91, 94, 112, 141
  See also narrative summary

exposition, 10–12, 31–37
  cumbersome, 31–32, 34–35
  in dialogue, 31–32, 103, 112
  in interior monologue, 32–34
  narrative summary for, 10
  showing vs. telling, 35–37

Faulkner, William, 218
  As I Lay Dying, 219
  The Reivers, 219

figures of speech, 203–4, 208
  voice and, 219–20, 221–28

films. *See* screenwriting

Final Witness (S. Tolkien), 99

first-person narrator, 41–43, 213–14, 229–32
  different characters as, 43, 229–32
  examples of, 41–42
  interior monologue mechanics for, 126–27, 128, 129–31
  plot development limitations with, 42–43

Fitzgerald, F. Scott
  The Great Gatsby, 6–7, 15–16, 17–18, 96–98, 246–47

flashbacks, 24, 27–28

Flight (Dorf), 76–77
formal dialogue, 100–104, 106–7, 167
formulaic novel, 187
frame story device, 12
fresh eyes
    manuscript review with, 1, 2, 74–75,
      176

Gallahue, John
    The Jesuit, 62–63
Games of the Hangman (O'Reilly),
    34–35
García Márquez, Gabriel, 88
Gardner, John
    On Becoming a Novelist, 1, 214
Gilchrist, Ellen
    The Annunciation, 138–39, 154–55,
      253–54
Gone With the Wind (Mitchell), 205–6
Gordon, Mary
    The Company of Women, 43,
      200–202, 229–32
Grafton, Sue
    M Is for Murder, 129–30
Great Gatsby, The (Fitzgerald), 6–7,
    15–16, 17–18
    dialogue exercise, 96–98, 246–47
Green, Hannah
    I Never Promised You a Rose Garden,
      169
Greene, Graham
    Monsignor Quixote, 29–30
    The Power and the Glory, 216

hack writing, 127, 193, 198–99
Happy All the Time (Colwin), 182
Hemingway, Ernest, 232
historical fiction, 10–12
Hoffman, Alice
    Practical Magic, 53–56
Huckleberry Finn (Twain), 109, 110

imagery
    beats and, 146
    character's use of, 202–4, 208
    voice and, 221–28
imagination
    reliance on reader's, 68, 69, 147, 204,
      206, 208
immediacy, 8–10, 12

I Never Promised You a Rose Garden
    (Green), 169
-ing construction, 193–95, 208
insecure writing, 200–201, 208
interior monologue, 64, 116–39, 148
    balance in, 122
    caveats about, 122–24, 127–28
    as characterization device, 33, 117–18
    as character's emotions portrayal
      device, 57, 116–17
    checklist, 134
    dialogue interruptions with, 118,
      121–22
    emotions portrayal with, 57, 64, 116–
      17
    exercises, 135–39
    exercises' answers, 250–54
    as exposition, 32–34
    first person and, 126–27, 128,
      129–31
    italics device, 126, 127–28, 134
    mechanics of, 122–31, 134
    narrative distance and, 124, 127, 128,
      131–33, 134
    paragraphing of, 128, 134
    pitfalls in writing, 117–22
    quotation marks and, 122
    repetition overuse in, 180–81
    rewards of, 133
    thinker attributions and, 124–26,
      127, 134, 141, 192
internal dialogue, 127, 128
intimacy
    advantages of, 51
    choice of voice and, 41–42, 47, 49,
      50–51, 77, 116
    interior monologue and, 128–29
    proportion and, 77
    shifting viewpoint and, 52
italics
    insecure writing and, 200–202, 208
    as interior monologue device, 126,
      127–28, 134
"I" voice. *See* first-person narrator

James, Henry, 8, 232
James, P. D.
    Devices and Desires, 73–74
    A Taste for Death, 139, 254
Jesuit, The (Gallahue), 62–63

Jones, Diana Wynne, 35–37
Joyce, James
    Portrait of the Artist as a Young Man,
        124–26, 219–20
jump-cuts, film and television, 68

Keillor, Garrison
    Leaving Home, 172–73
Killshot (Leonard), 105
King, Stephen
    Dreamcatcher, 149–50
Kingsolver, Barbara
    Animal Dreams, 151–52
Kirk, Captain (fictional character),
        25–26

La Brava (Leonard), 163–64
Langton, Jane
    Divine Inspiration, 44–46
language
    elevated, 202–4, 219–20, 221–28
    point of view and, 48, 50–51, 64
    profanity and obscenity use, 206, 208
    See also dialogue
large-scale repetition, 184–87
large-scale showing, 5–15
lazy writing, 84, 85, 87, 127, 198
Leatherstocking novels (J. F. Cooper),
        188
Leaving Home (Keillor), 172–73
le Carré, John
    The Constant Gardener, 216–18
    The Russia House, 153–54
    The Secret Pilgrim, 110–11, 138,
        165–66, 253
Lehman-Haupt, Christopher, 70–71
length
    paragraphing and, 162, 166, 172
    repetition and, 175–91
Leonard, Elmore
    Killshot, 105
    La Brava, 163–64
    Touch, 60–61
Letourneau's Used Auto Parts (Chute), 49
linespaces, 60–61, 64, 204
literary homages, 218–19
Lonesome Dove (McMurtry), 40–41, 43,
        52, 55
Los Angeles Times, 18–19
Lovelife (Searle), 71–72

Lovely Bones, The (Sebold), 214–15
Ludlum, Robert
    The Bourne Ultimatum, 82
-ly adverbs
    avoidance for sophisticated effect,
        197–99, 208
    avoidance in dialogue, 86–88, 91,
        94–95, 112, 141

manipulation of reader, 76
manuscripts
    drafts of, 207
    ear review of, 107–8
    fresh-eye review of, 1, 2, 74–75,
        176
    proportion errors in, 74
    reasons for self-editing of, 2–3
    review for repetition in, 188–89
    white space in, 167, 172
    See also writing
McBain, Ed, 110–11
McCrumb, Sharyn
    The Ballad of Frankie Silver, 42
McGrath, Patrick, 175
McMurtry, Larry, 57
    Lonesome Dove, 40–41, 52, 55
Melville, Herman
    Moby-Dick, 70, 213–14, 228–29
    Omoo, 213, 214, 228–29
metaphors, 203–4, 208
Middlemarch (Eliot), 43–44
minimalism
    natural voice and, 219–20
minor characters, 52, 197
misdirection in dialogue, 104–5
M Is for Murder (Grafton), 129–30
Miss Marple mysteries (Christie), 76
Mitchell, Margaret
    Gone With the Wind, 205–6
Moby-Dick (Melville)
    proportion and, 70
    voice and, 213–14, 228–29
monologue. *See* interior monologue
Monsignor Quixote (Greene), 29–30
Morrison, Toni
    The Bluest Eye, 147–48
movies. *See* screenwriting
multiple voices
    point of view and, 229–32
Murder at the Vicarage (Christie), 76

Murphy, Gloria
  Down Will Come Baby, 166–67
  Nightshade, 186–87

narration, 107–8
  cliché variation in, 197
  frame story device, 12
  proportion and, 72–73, 77–79
  reading aloud for stiffness in, 108–9,
    112
  rhythm in, 12–13
  subtle sex scene conventions and,
    204–5
  See also point of view; voice
narrative distance, 55–56
  choice of voice and, 41–42, 48–52,
    64
  control of, 52, 61, 131
  deciding on amount of, 50, 51–52,
    55–56
  interior monologue and, 124, 127,
    128, 131–33, 134
  stunning effects with, 61–62
  See also intimacy
narrative rhythm, 12–13
narrative summary, 5–22
  characterization and, 23–26
  checklist, 19–20
  examples of, 5, 7, 23–24
  exercises, 20–22
  exercises' answers, 235–39
  for exposition, 10
  overuse of, 8, 9
  pitfalls of, 10
  uses of, 10–11, 12–15
narrative voice. *See* voice
narrator. *See* point of view; voice
Nathan, Robert Stuart, 34–35
New York Times, The, 70–71, 99, 175
New York Times Book Review, The, 82
Nicholson, Geoff, 99
Nightshade (Murphy), 186–87
Nimoy, Leonard, 25–26
nineteenth-century novels, 43–44, 70,
  213–14

Oates, Joyce Carol, 44
objectivity, in manuscript review, 1, 2,
  74–75, 176
obscenity, use of, 206, 208

observation
  beats and, 152
omniscient narrator, 41, 43–47, 62–63,
    64
  advantages and drawbacks of, 46–47
  shift to specific third-person, 62–63
Omoo (Melville), 213, 214, 228–29
On Becoming a Novelist (Gardner), 1,
    214
on-line publishing, 2
O'Reilly, Victor
  Games of the Hangman, 34–35

pacing, 51
  dialogue and, 144
  paragraphing and, 163–67
  See also tension
paragraphing, 160–74
  avoidance of lengthy, 162, 172
  balance in, 172
  checklist, 172
  dialogue and, 94, 95, 162, 163,
    167–68
  exercises, 172–74
  exercises' answers, 257–59
  for interior monologue, 128, 134
  length and, 162, 166, 172
  pacing and, 163–67
  plot development and, 166
  repetition and, 175–76, 188
  tension and frequency of, 162–64
Pargeter, Edith
  The Eighth Champion of Christendom,
    220–21
Paulson, Tim
  The Real World, 183–84
personal appearance
  description of character's, 24–25
personality traits
  portrayal of, 25
perspective
  first-person voice and, 42–43
  omniscient voice and, 45–46, 47
Phillips, Julia
  *You'll Never Eat Lunch in This Town
    Again*, 185–86
physical action descriptions. *See* beats
physical description, 24–25
plot development
  atmosphere and, 73–74

plot development (*continued*)
  figures of speech and, 203–4, 208
  first-person voice as limiting, 42–43
  formulaic, 187
  objective review of manuscript and, 75
  paragraph length and, 166
  point of view shifts for, 60–61
  proportion and, 72–73, 75–77, 79, 80
  repetition and, 176, 187, 189
  subplots and, 74, 80
poetic prose, 202–4, 219–20, 221–22
point of view, 40–66
  characterization with, 29–30, 43, 52
  of characters, 29–30, 43, 48–66, 68, 77, 80, 91–92, 229–32
  checklist, 64
  early establishment of, 59–60
  emotions and, 57–59
  exercises, 65–66
  exercises' answers, 240–44
  first-person, 41–43, 126–27, 129–31
  importance of, 64
  interior monologue attribution and, 124–26, 127, 130
  intimacy and, 41–42, 47, 49, 50–51, 77, 116
  multiple voices and, 229–32
  omniscient, 41, 43–47, 62–63
  overly detailed description and, 68, 77
  proportion and, 77–79, 80
  shifts in, 41, 43, 52–59, 60–61, 64
  speaker attribution and, 91–92
  sticking with, 52
  style and, 219
  third-person, 41, 47–50, 64
  word choice and syntax and, 48, 64
  See also voice
polysyllabic words, 103–4
Portrait of the Artist as a Young Man (Joyce)
  interior monologue and, 124–26
  poetic prose and, 219–20
Power and the Glory, The (Greene), 216
Practical Magic (Hoffman), 53–56
Praise Singer, The (Renault), 130–31
pretentiousness, literary, 219
Price of Milk and Money, The (Cottle), 111

print on demand, 2
profanity, 206, 208
proportion, 67–81
  atmosphere and, 73–74
  in beats use, 148–49
  characters and, 72–74, 77–79, 80
  checklist, 80
  cutting effects on, 71–72
  cutting to achieve, 73, 74
  detail overuse and, 67–69, 77, 79
  digressions and, 70, 74, 75
  emotions and, 1–2
  exercises, 81
  exercises' answers, 244–45
  in interior monologue, 122
  intimacy and, 77
  manuscript review for judging, 74–75
  narration and, 72–73, 77–79
  in paragraphing, 172
  personal interests interfering with, 69, 70, 79, 80
  plot development and, 72–73, 75–77, 79, 80
  point of view and, 77–79, 80
  repetition and, 184
  sources of problems, 67–73, 79
  texture and, 74
  use of, 75–77, 79
  voice and, 222
publishing industry, 2
punctuation
  as action bridgers, 68–69
  of dialogue, 93–94, 102, 103, 199
  of short sentences, 199, 208

quotation marks
  for emphasis, 200
  interior monologue and, 122

Rashomon technique, 182
readers
  condescending to, 84, 85, 177
  dialogue explanations and, 84, 85, 86
  elevated language and, 222, 225
  emotions of, 10
  engagement of, 8–9, 10, 19, 219
  manipulation of, 76
  reliance on imagination of, 68, 69, 147, 204, 206, 208

reading aloud
  for character's voice, 232–33
  of descriptions, 107–8
  for dialogue sound, 107–9, 112, 151
  for narration stiffness, 108–9, 112
  for voice, 228
real time, 7, 19, 31
Real World, The (Paulson), 183–84
Reasonable Madness, A (Dorf)
  beats and, 140–43, 146, 148
  repetition and, 190–91
Reivers, The (Faulkner), 219
Renault, Mary
  The Praise Singer, 130–31
repetition, 175–91, 192
  of action, 14–15
  from book to book, 187
  of brand names, 179–80
  for characterization, 176
  of characters, 184, 186–87
  checklist, 188–89
  in dialogue, 180
  for effect, 182–83
  of effects, 175–79
  exercises, 189–91
  exercises' answers, 259–61
  intentional vs. unintentional, 182
  in interior monologues, 180–81
  large-scale, 184–87
  paragraphing and, 175–76, 188
  plot development and, 176, 187, 189
  problem example, 183–84
  reviewing manuscript for, 188–89
  small-scale, 175–84
  in unconscious word choices, 181–82, 189
resist urge to explain (R.U.E.), 16, 20, 84, 86
review of manuscript. *See* manuscripts
rhythm
  beats and, 149–51, 158
  in description, 107
  in dialogue, 107, 110, 149–51, 158
  mechanics of, 171
  in narrative, 12–13
  variation in, 12, 171
Rice, Anne
  The Witching Hour, 175

Robinson, Jill
  Dr. Rocksinger and the Age of Longing, 144–45
R.U.E. (resist urge to explain), 16, 20, 84, 86
Russia House, The (le Carré), 153–54

said
  annoying alternatives to, 82
  as dialogue mechanical device, 88, 90–91
  replacement with beats, 92–93
scenes
  action and, 8, 51–52
  building tension in, 61–63
  characteristics of, 7–9
  length of, 171, 172
  linespace insertion in, 60–61, 64
  metaphor as distraction from, 203–4
  multiple elements in, 183
  narrative summary vs., 8, 9, 12–13, 14, 15–16, 24
  paragraphing and, 171, 172
  pitfalls in writing, 12–14
  point of view and, 51–52, 59–60
  proportion in, 67–81
  in real time, 7, 19, 131
  rhythm of, 171
  settings of, 7–8
  about sex, 204–5, 208
science fiction, 10, 12, 35–37
screenwriting, 104, 107, 182
  jump-cuts, 68
  visuality and, 116
Searle, Judith
  Lovelife, 71–72
Sebold, Alice
  The Lovely Bones, 214–15
Secret Pilgrim, The (le Carré), 138, 253
  character's speech pattern and, 110–11
  paragraphing and, 165–66
See, Carolyn, 183–84
sentences
  distinctive, 218
  in formal dialogue, 167
  fragments in dialogue, 101–2, 112
  repetition and, 175
  strung on commas, 199, 208
  tension-building, 162–63

settings, 7–8
  beats and, 146
sex scenes, 204–6, 208
short sentences, 199, 208, 218
showing, 5–22
  dialogue and, 85
  large-scale, 5–15
  small-scale, 15–19
  telling vs., 5–22, 24, 26, 35–37, 85,
    160–61, 162, 188, 199
small-scale repetition, 175–84
small-scale showing, 15–19
Smith, Lee
  Black Mountain Breakdown, 78–79
sophistication, 192–212
  as construction, 193–95, 208
  checklist, 208
  comma usage and, 199, 208
  dialogue effects, 199
  effortless writing and, 207–8
  exercises, 211–12
  -ing construction and, 193–95, 208
  narrative voice and, 221
  poetic imagery and, 202–4, 208
  sex scenes and, 204–6, 208
speaker attributions, 88–93, 95, 112,
    141
  beats replacing, 85, 92–93, 95
  dispensing with, 92, 95
  interior monologue and, 124–26,
    127, 134, 192
  placement of, 91
  point of view and, 91–92
  said and, 88, 90–91
  word choice and, 89
speech patterns, 101–12
  distinctive voices of characters and,
    232
  representation in dialogue, 110–11
spelling
  dialect and, 110, 111, 112
Spiritual Quests (Buechner), 232
Spock, Mr. (fictional character),
    25–26
Spy magazine, 185
Star Trek series (television), 25–26
Stein, Sol
  The Best Revenge, 43
stereotypes, characters as, 186
stilted dialogue, 103

stylistic devices
  changes in fashion of, 187–88,
    209–10
  homage imitations of, 219
  insecure, 200–202
  point of view and, 219
  repetition as, 189
  sex scenes and, 204–6
  sophisticated effects from, 193–212
  tacky, 200
  voice vs., 219, 232
subplots, 74, 80
syntax, point of view and, 48, 64

tape recorder, 107
Taste for Death, A (P. D. James), 139, 254
television. See screenwriting
telling, 5–22
  by characters, 26
  by dialogue, 85
  large-scale, 5–15
  showing vs., 5–22, 24, 26, 35–37, 85,
    160–61, 162, 188, 199
  small-scale, 15–19
tension
  beats used for, 153–57
  brief scenes and chapters for, 171
  devices for building, 61–63, 153–57,
    162–64
  frequent paragraphing and, 162–64
  See also pacing
texture of writing, 12, 51
  proportion and, 74
thinker attributions, 124–26, 127, 134,
    141, 192
third-person narrator, 41, 47–50, 64
  advantages of, 47
  character discrepancy and, 48
  interior monologue and, 127, 134
  omniscient narration shift to, 62–63
thoughts of characters. See interior
    monologue
thrillers
  frequent paragraphing and, 163–64
time
  flashback problems and, 28
  scene events and, 7, 19, 31
Tolkien, Simon
  Final Witness, 99
Tolstoy, Leo, 232

Touch (Leonard), 60–61
transitions, 68
    linespace insertion and, 60–61, 64
Treasure Hunt (Buechner), 153, 167–68
Trollope, Anthony, 232
Twain, Mark
    Cooper's Leatherstocking novels
        review by, 188
    Huckleberry Finn, 109, 110
Tyler, Anne
    Dinner at the Homesick Restaurant,
        155–57, 169–71
typeface changes, 127. *See also* italics

unconscious repetitions, 181–82, 189
uninterrupted dialogue, 147–48

verbs
    action and, 89
    speaker attribution pitfalls, 88–89,
        112
    weak vs. strong, specific, 197, 198
viewpoint character. *See* point of view
villains, 186, 186–87, 189
Vivaldi, Antonio, 10–12
voice, 213–34
    authorial interconnection with
        character's, 214–21
    of characters, 48, 214–15, 221–28,
        232–33
    character's distinctive, 229–33
    checklist and exercises, 234
    of description vs. character's, 48
    development of, 218–19, 228–29,
        232–33
    in dialogue, 107–8
    distinctive and authoritative, 218, 228
    elevated language and, 202–4,
        221–28
    first-person, 41–43, 213–14, 229–32
    imagery and, 202–4
    interior monologue and, 124–26,
        127, 130
    intimacy and, 41–42, 47, 49
    literary homages and, 218–19
    minimalism and, 219–20
    narrative distance and, 41–42, 48–52,
        64
    obtrusive exposition in, 31

omniscient, 41, 43–47, 62–63, 64
    point of view and, 48–50
    proportion and, 222
    showing vs. telling and, 199
    style vs., 219, 232
    third-person, 41, 47–50, 64
    See also point of view

weak writing, 84, 85, 87, 127, 198
Welty, Eudora
    "The Wide Net," 152–53
white spaces, 167, 172
"Wide Net, The" (Welty), 152–53
Witching Hour, The (Rice), 175
Wolf and the Dove, The (Woodiwiss),
        209, 261
Woodiwiss, Kathleen E.
    The Wolf and the Dove, 209, 261
word choice
    cliché avoidance, 196–97
    in dialogue, 103–4, 110, 112
    point of view and, 48, 64
    profanity and, 206
    speaker attribution and, 89
    unconscious repetitions in, 181–82,
        189
writing
    amateur giveaways, 9–10, 89, 219
    book to book repetitions in, 187
    cliché avoidance, 196–97
    constructions that weaken, 193–95
    distinctive voice and, 218–19, 228
    editing vs., 3–4
    effect of effortless, 207–8
    hack commonalities in, 127, 193,
        198–99
    insecure, 200–201, 208
    lazy or weak, 84, 85, 87, 127, 198
    pretentious, 219
    reading aloud benefits for, 107–9,
        112, 151, 228, 232–33
    texture of, 12, 51, 74
    top books about, 264–67
    See also editing; manuscripts
writing groups, 3
Wuthering Heights (E. Brontë), 215–16

*You'll Never Eat Lunch in This Town
    Again* (Phillips), 185–86

ABOUT THE AUTHORS

RENNI BROWNE, once senior editor for William Morrow and other companies, left mainstream publishing in 1980 to found The Editorial Department, a national book-editing company (www.editorialdepartment.net). A founder of the Lost State Writer's Conference in Greeneville, Tennessee, she publishes articles and book reviews in *Appalachian Life* magazine.

DAVE KING is a contributing editor at *Writer's Digest*. He also works as an independent editor in his home in rural Ashfield, Massachusetts, and on-line at daveking edits.com. Many of his magazine pieces on the art of writing have been anthologized in *The Complete Handbook of Novel Writing* and in *The Writer's Digest Writing Clinic*.